Book 2 in SAP FICO Books

SAP FINANCIAL ACCOUNTING

Fast Track Your Career

As an SAP ACCOUNTANT

Murugesan Ramaswamy

SAP FINANCIAL ACCOUNTING v 1.0

https://sapficouser.com

ꝏꝏ

Who can benefit from this book?

SAP Financial Accounting (SFACTG) is for the SAP Accountants to gain FI module expertise.

SFACTG book empowers you with knowledge on **master data to transaction postings and reports generation** in SAP GL, AR & AP. Even if you are a beginner, the lessons are laid out clearly to guide you.

Study Plan

Chapter 1: The System Concept of a Document, for a **strong foundation** as an SAP Accountant.

Chapter 2 to 4: Lessons on master records to keep the **accounting records in the best form**.

Chapter 5 & 6: Document posting lessons that save a ton of your time in your daily tasks in the system.

Chapter 7: Document clearing to keep your **transaction records tidy** and avoid unwanted stress working with the system.

Chapter 8: A lesson on system reports, generating the **system reports is no more a mystery**; the chapter guides you to get the reports you need.

What this book is NOT

SFACTG *does not explain SAP configuration steps*. However, FI consultants who want to learn how to get the accounting tasks done in the system will find this book helpful.

Book 1 in SAP FICO Books

You can learn SAP FICO basics —navigation, fundamental concepts, and tips and tricks in SAP FICO BEGINNER'S HANDBOOK:

https://sapficouscr.com/home/sapficobooks/

Join Facebook Group

Join our **Facebook group** dedicated to SAP accounting professionals to ask questions and share their knowledge following the link:

https://sapficouser.com/home/facebook-group/

SAP Version

This book follows SAP ECC 6.0 version.

About the Author

The author of SFACTG is a Chartered Accountant from India. He has over thirty-year functional experience in Finance & Accounts in different business verticals, including Engineering, Manufacturing, Trading, and Real Estate.

He has experience in SAP implementations in the SAP FICO domain in various roles such as Core Team Member, Project Manager, and Process Owner. He is a passionate FICO Accounting professional who wants to guide the SAP Accountants to achieve their best with the system.

∞∞

Table of Contents

∞∞

CHAPTER 1

The System Concept of a Document

The document is a piece of evidence of a business transaction. In the SAP system, documents are the system record of transaction entries.

Let's understand the document from a system perspective for a fundamental knowledge of the SAP Financial Accounting module.

If you've been using the system for some time, you may want to skip this chapter. However, please read the contents of the chapter once; you may find the narrative from a new angle.

Chapter Contents

1. The Document

This topic narrates how the SAP system identifies the 'documents' and facilitates document classification, storage, and retrieval.

i) Account Types

The system posts documents to the ledger accounts. Therefore, let us now learn the ledger accounts code in the system.

The system classifies ledger accounts with one-letter 'account type' codes. Here are the account type codes in the system:

Account Types	Description
S	General Ledger Accounts
D	Customers Accounts
K	Vendors Accounts
A	Asset Accounts
M	Materials Ledger Accounts

The system uses the account type codes in various system outputs. Therefore, becoming familiar with the account type codes will help you work with the system more efficiently. Also, the one-letter account type code is used to create *two-letter document types*, which we will learn next.

ii) Document Types

Document types are the two-letter codes for document classification.

The most often used document types are:

Document type	Type Description
AA	Asset posting
SA	Accounting document
DR	Customer invoice
DZ	Customer payment
KR	Vendor invoice
KZ	Vendor payment

Learning by heart the frequently used document types goes a long way in gaining comfort working with the system.

Account Types & Document Types: the Relationship

You might have already noticed, the **first letters** in the two-letter 'document types' are the 'account type codes.'

For example, the Asset Accounting document type is AA; the first letter A refers to the Asset Accounting account type code. Similarly, DR for Customer Invoice, the first letter D refers to the customer accounts.

Understanding how the account type codes relate to document type codes helps you to remember them easily.

We understand 'documents' in the system. We'll discuss the document in detail on the next following topics.

∞

2. The Document Header

Each document has header information and line items.

Document header contains information that is common to the entire document. Let us learn each field of the document header and its significance.

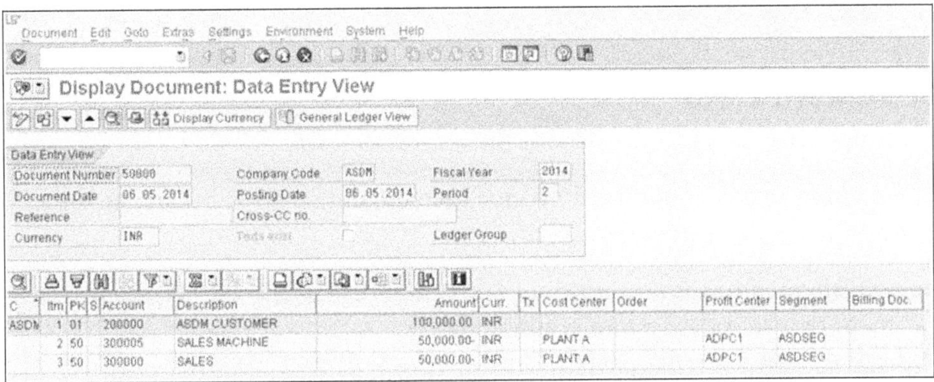

Itm	PK	Account	Description	Amount	Curr.	Cost Center	Profit Center	Segment
1	01	200000	ASDM CUSTOMER	100,000.00	INR			
2	50	300005	SALES MACHINE	50,000.00-	INR	PLANT A	ADPC1	ASDSEG
3	50	300000	SALES	50,000.00-	INR	PLANT A	ADPC1	ASDSEG

i) Document Number

Every Document in the system is identified & controlled by a unique document number auto-generated by the system. The system generates the document numbers for each document type from a predefined number range.

Document type and document number help in the hard copy documents classification and sequential filing.

Let's understand this point with an illustration.

Consider, for Asset Accounting documents, the system generates numbers from a specific range: 12001 to 12500; Then, for accounting documents, numbers are generated from a number range of 12501 to 13000.

Numbers run sequentially for documents of each document type. Therefore, we can file the hard copy documents of individual document types separately.

ii) Company Code

The company code represents the legal reporting structure in the SAP System.

We prepare the year-end Balance Sheet and Profit and Loss Account and get them audited, and file with the regulatory authorities *for a company code.*

In the system, the company code is a four-digit number such as 1000, 2000. Company codes can also be alphanumerical such as ABC1, ABC2.

iii) The Fiscal Year

The fiscal year is the period for which we prepare the Annual Financial Statements, get them audited, and file them with the regulatory authorities.

In India, the fiscal year is twelve months, from 1st Apr to 31st Mar. The fiscal year follows the calendar year, from 1st Jan to 31st Dec, in the US and several other countries.

iv) Document Date

The document date refers to the date of the *original document.*

As an illustration, when you enter a vendor invoice, the *invoice date in the documents received from the vendor* is the document date.

Document date assumes importance as the system calculates the payment terms from the document date in most system configurations.

v) Posting Date

We choose the posting date during data entry, provided that the date falls within the open posting period.

Usually, by default, the system date is the posting date. However, we have to change the system's proposed posting date when the posting period is not open for that date.

vi) Posting Period

We are familiar with the posting period. Nevertheless, let me quickly refresh the concept for the benefit of beginners.

The posting period is the system design to put an end date for finalizing the accounting data for the monthly management reports.

Posting periods usually coincide with the calendar months. Thus, there are twelve posting periods within a fiscal year.

The system does not permit data entry in a closed posting period.

We close the posting period at the end of each calendar month to prepare and submit the internal management reports.

vii) Document Entry Date

The document entry date is the **system date** of data entry. We don't input the document entry date; the system automatically records them during the data entry.

What is the benefit of the document entry date?

We can extract a list of documents entered in the system on a particular date. As an illustration, we can generate a list of all documents *entered on*, say Friday, 31st Jul 2020, when we want to check them.

viii) Reference Field

The reference field is for entering the **external reference**.

Let's understand the external reference with an example: In a vendor invoice, the invoice number is the external reference.

When we enter a vendor invoice in the system, we input the vendor invoice number in the 'reference' field.

How is the 'reference field' helpful?

We can have the reference field content printed in the vendors' account statement, thus making their life easier. Besides, we can query the system for a vendor invoice with a vendor invoice number.

ix) Currency

There are two currency types in the system:

a) The company code currency, and
b) The document currency.

a) The Company Code Currency

The company code currency is the legal tender of the country where the company is registered.

As an illustration, the company code currency of a company operating in India is INR.

A company prepares the year-end financial statements in the company code currency.

b) The Document Currency

Document currency is the currency of the external document.

For example, consider a document in INR; INR is the document currency. For a company in India, in this case, both the company code currency and the document currency are the same.

Consider a scenario for a company in India receiving an invoice in USD for an import transaction from the USA. In this case, USD is the document currency.

∞

3. Posting Keys

Posting keys are the control keys for the document entry in the system. The posting keys are two-digit numerical numbers.

During a document entry, we enter the document header info and then enter the line items. To enter the line items, we have to input the **posting keys.**

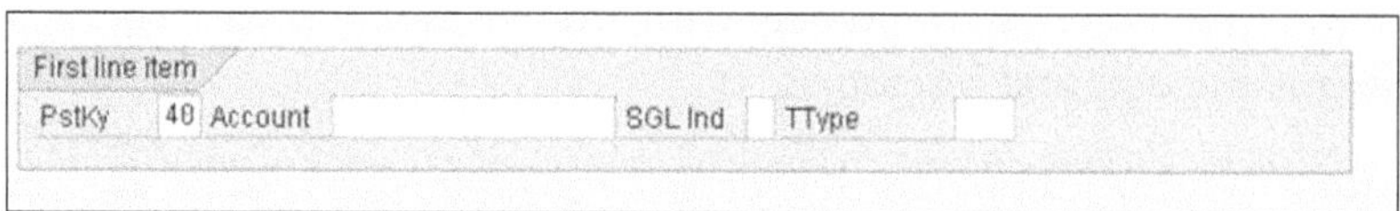

The posting key for a line item determines:

1) Debit or Credit posting,
2) Posting to the GL or AR or AP, and
3) The Transaction Type, such as the customer invoice or the customer payment posting.

Some of the often used posting keys are:

Posting Key	**PstKy function**
40	GL Debit entry
50	GL Credit entry
01	Accounts Receivable Customer Invoice, a debit entry
31	Accounts Payable Vendor Invoice, a credit entry.

∞

4. Customer and Vendor Normal & Special Transactions

The system classifies *customer and vendor transaction* entries into normal and special transactions.

Customer accounts normal transactions are sales and payment receipts against the sales. Vendor accounts normal transactions are purchases and payments against the purchases.

Transactions other than the normal transactions are special transactions.

For example, customer and vendor advance payments are special transactions.

Also, non-financial transactions, such as payment requests, guarantees are special transactions.

We will learn how to post 'normal' and 'special' transactions, and the GL accounts for posting them in the next topic.

5. Reconciliation and Special GL Accounts

The system links the GL and a sub-ledger through unique GL accounts, namely, the reconciliation accounts and special GL accounts.

Reconciliation accounts are the GL Accounts for the customer and vendor normal transactions; **special GL accounts** are for the special transactions.

For example, the 'Trade Receivables Account' in the GL is the reconciliation account for the accounts receivable. The system accounts for 'normal' transactions posted in the customers' accounts in the GL via the Trade Receivables Account.

Similarly, the system posts vendors' accounts normal transactions in the GL via the Trade Payables Account.

Why do we need Special GL Accounts?

We need Special GL Accounts because we've to report the special transactions separately in the Balance Sheet.

As an example, we need to report the customer advances in the Balance Sheet separately. This is possible by accounting for the customers' and vendors' advance payments in Special GL Accounts in the GL.

The system posts the customers' and vendors' special transactions to the special GL accounts using the special GL indicators, which we will learn next.

Special GL Indicators

Special GL indicators are the control keys for posting customers' and vendors' special transactions.

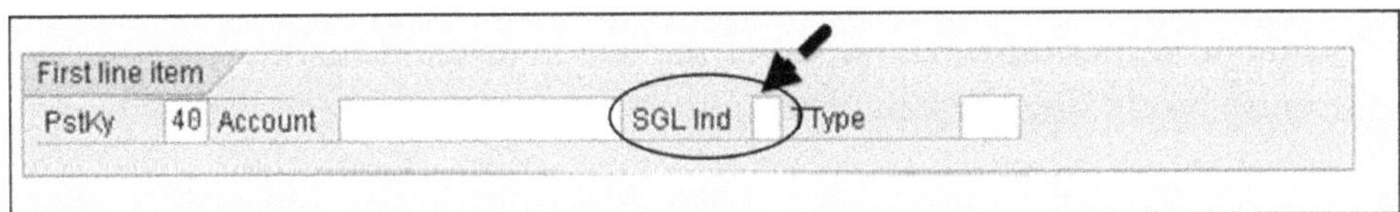

When we post a 'special' transaction, we have to select a 'special GL indicator' after entering the posting key.

Based on the special GL indicator, the system posts that transaction to the special GL account in the GL.

To sum up, the special GL indicator is a posting control key, in addition to the posting key. Thus, entering transactions using the special GL indicator enables the system to record the special entries under separate GL Accounts called special GL accounts.

There are separate special GL accounts for every kind of special transaction.

Some of the special GL indicators and the special GL accounts in the system are:

Spl. GL Indicator	Special GL Accounts
A	Down payments on current assets account
D	Discounts account
H	Security deposits account

∞

6. Document Posting Essentials

In this topic, we will discuss helpful data entry features in the system. This topic is for an absolute beginner with the SAP system.

i) Holding a Document

Holding a document can be explained easily with an illustration.

During data entry, you may have to interrupt your document entry midway for many reasons. Maybe your boss is calling you for an urgent meeting, or some critical data for the posting is missing. However, you have completed a substantial portion of the entry.

In such a scenario, **holding** is a handy functionality. You can manually assign a temporary number as the **held document number** and HOLD the document for later updating and **posting**.

ii) Simulating before Posting

Before you post a transaction in the system, you want to view how the transaction gets posted as debit and credit items.

Enter document header information, enter the line items, and before you post, you can check the entry by clicking the 'Simulate' button

The system displays the transaction as it would get posted in the system: document header, GL account codes, debit, credit line items, and the automatic posting line items.

Thus, simulation is a **handy tool for reviewing** before posting, whenever you are posting a transaction with multiple line items or a transaction that you expect with automatic posting line items.

iii) Parking a Document

Document parking is an intermediary stage of a document entry and posting function. We will now learn the scenarios where 'document parking' is helpful.

a) Payment against Parked Documents

You can release payment against a parked document using the 'payment request' function.

Payment against a parked document may be needed when you have to make that payment to avail of a discount, but you don't have enough information to complete the posting.

You can create a payment request against the parked document, and the automatic payment program will pick that payment request and process the payment.

Please refer to the topic 'Partial Payments' (page no. 48) under Chapter 5 Document Posting TCodes discussing creating and using payment requests.

b) Tax Returns

Preparing your tax returns is another scenario where the document parking function is useful.

We have to file the tax returns within the deadline.

However, it may so happen that we could not post some of the transactions belonging to the tax return period due to incomplete information. In this scenario, we may enter and keep such transactions in the system in the parked status and compile the tax returns.

We can generate reports with the parked and the regular documents to compile the tax returns and file them in time.

Necessary Precaution in Using Document Parking

The system generates the document number from the **Document Number Range** when you park a document.

So, be careful if you have to delete a parked document. When you delete a parked document, the system deletes the 'document number' also.

The system does not use the document number of the deleted parked document for a new document, resulting in a missing document number.

Later, during the audit, the auditors may raise a query for the missing document number.

iv) Posting with Reference Document

Document posting can be effortless if you choose a similar document already posted in the system and enter that selected document as a 'reference document' when you post.

Posting with a reference document is the simplest method of document posting minimizing data entry mistakes.

TCodes for Posting with Reference

- ✓ FB50 - Enter G/L Account Document
- ✓ F-02 - General Posting
- ✓ FB70 - Customer Invoice
- ✓ FB60 - Vendor Invoice

Main Menu: Go To >> Post with Reference

Enter the Reference Document Number, Company Code, and Fiscal Year.

Please don't select any options under the 'Flow Control' and complete your posting for the Posting with Reference.

∞

We have covered the system concept of a document and the system design for posting them. In the following three chapters, we will learn the financial accounting master records.

∞∞

CHAPTER 2

GL Master Records

The system is a storehouse of business records. System records are of two types: The master records and the transaction records.

Master records provide the system key information necessary for the data entry, data analysis, evaluation, and reporting. Master records ensure processing transactions in a controlled environment.

Compared to transaction records, master records are permanent. They are not associated with a calendar date. Each master record links to multiple transaction records over a period of time.

We have three chapters, chapters 2, 3 & 4, for learning financial accounting master records.

In this chapter, we will learn GL master records.

Chapter Contents

∞

1. The Chart of Accounts

The Chart of Accounts is the comprehensive list of GL accounts. In the SAP system, usually, we have two CoAs:

i) Operating Chart of Accounts and
ii) Group Chart of Accounts.

i) Operating Chart of Accounts

The Chart of Accounts that we use for our daily tasks is the operating CoA.

Our daily tasks include transaction posting, report generation, and new account creation.

Operating Chart of Accounts fulfills the country-specific and legal reporting requirements.

For example, an Indian company's operating Chart of Accounts has regular GL accounts and India-specific accounts such as GST input and output tax accounts. Thus, the operating Chart of Accounts for companies in India will be different from the operating Chart of Accounts for companies in the USA.

ii) Group Chart of Accounts

The Chart of Accounts used for group-level reporting is the Group Chart of Accounts.

Thus, the group Chart of Accounts is used for preparing the consolidated Balance Sheet and Profit & Loss Account by the holding company.

For example, consider a company ABC Ltd in India is a subsidiary of ABC Holding Inc. in the USA.

In this scenario, ABC Ltd will have an India-specific Chart of Accounts as its operating Chart of Accounts and a second USA-specific Chart of Accounts as the group Chart of Accounts.

∞

2. Company Code

The company code refers to the legal reporting structure.

We prepare the Balance Sheet and Profit and Loss Account for the year-end audit and later file with the regulatory bodies for a company code.

3. Business Area

The Business Area in the SAP System is an **organizational structure** independent of the company codes.

We can prepare a Balance Sheet and Profit & Loss Account for a Business Area like a company code.

The company codes are defined as per legal reporting requirements. Business Areas are configured around **business segments**, such as **product category or geographical location.**

Business Areas help prepare *segment reporting* under IFRS. Each reporting segment is configured as a Business Area.

However, the Business Area is not a preferred option in recent times as a reporting tool. Whatever benefits we may get from the Business Areas can be had from the **Profit Centers.**

So, don't be surprised in case if you find your SAP system is NOT configured with Business Area functionality.

∞

4. Creating a New GL Account

i) New GL Account in the Company Code

We want to create a new GL Account for a company code. The account code is already available in the Chart of Accounts.

Create with Reference Method

FSS0 - In Company Code

Main Menu option: GL Account >> Create with Reference

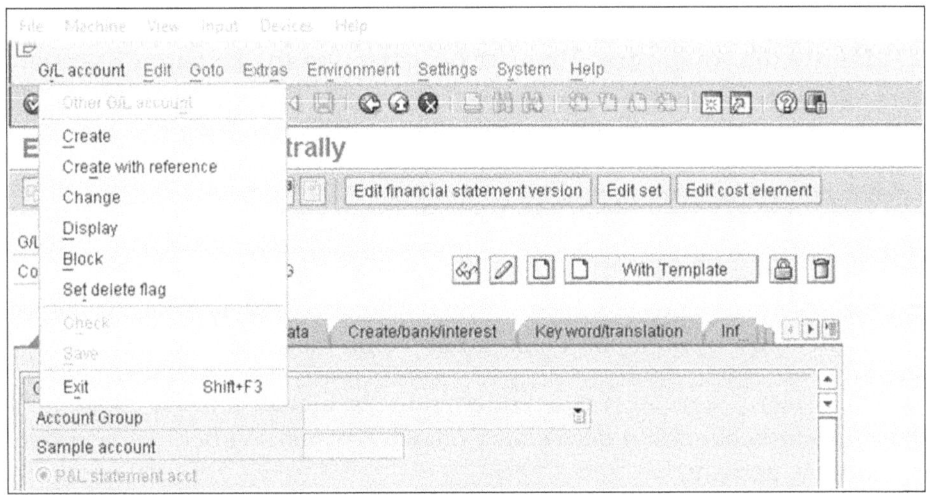

'Create with reference' is the simplest way of creating a new GL Account in the system.

We need a reference account. The **'reference account'** is an account already in the company code that is the closest cousin of the new account we want to create.

So, what is the advantage of the reference method?

As we give a reference account number, the system copies the reference account master data to the new account we create; thus, the new account creation is much easier.

Let's consider a scenario: We want to create a new 'Petty Cash Account.' Then, we choose an existing petty cash account number as the 'reference account.'

Another example, for creating a new bank account, we select an existing bank account as the reference account.

When we enter an existing GL Account as a 'reference,' the system defaults all the master data fields from the referenced account master.

We have the option to accept or make necessary changes to the values proposed by the system.

After reviewing the data populated in the account creation screen by the system, we can save it. The system displays a message to the effect a new account is created in the system.

ii) Create New GL Account in CoA & Comp. Code

FS00 - In Chart of Accounts & Company Codes

We learned to create an account in a company code that is already in the Chart of Accounts.

Consider a scenario, we need a GL Account, and we have to create it in the Chart of Accounts and the company code.

We can create a new account in the CoA and the company code in **four steps.**

Step 1: Identify the Reference Account & Determine the Account Number

Identify a 'reference account' for the new GL account to be created, as discussed in the first method.

Let us determine the account number.

Enter the TCode FS00, press the button - new account creation.

Use an F4 search in the create screen - account number field and search through the existing GL accounts to determine a unique number in the same account group.

For example, when you create a new GL account for a bank account, browse through the existing bank accounts and decide on a unique account number, the next one to an existing bank GL account.

Step 2: Enter TCode FS00

Create a new session following the menu path: System >> Create Session

Enter the TCode FS00 in the command line.

You have two fields in the initial screen.

1) GL Account: Type the new Account number you have determined and the account description. For example, account number 350370, description: 'Petty Cash - Branch Warehouse.'

2) Company Code: Enter the company code where you need the new account and press 'Enter.'

Step 3: Main Menu: GL Account >> Create with Reference

Enter the reference account number and its company code, and press Enter.

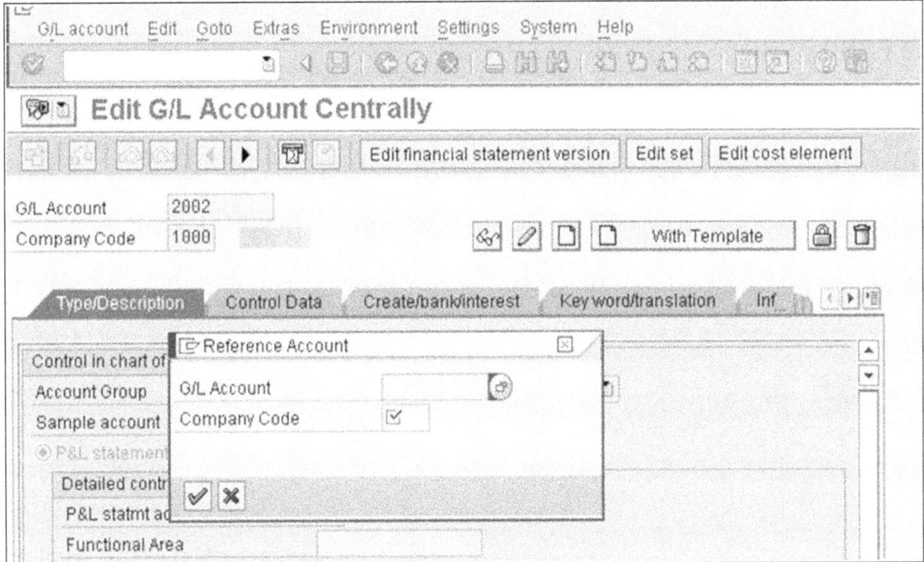

Step 4: Review, And Change as Required

The system populates the necessary fields from the referenced account data; we need to carefully review them and make changes as required for the new account and save them.

We've created the new account, both in the Chart of Accounts and in the company code.

∞

5. Blocking GL Accounts

We know master records remain in the system much longer, often more than a fiscal year. We also know master records control the system environment to record transactions in the system.

Any incorrect master record leads to inaccurate transaction records in the system. Hence it is essential to enter and maintain correct master records data.

In this context, we'll now learn how to block GL Accounts.

The TCodes

FS00 - In Chart of Accounts & Company Codes

FSS0 - In Company Code

Menu: GL Account >> Block

TCode FSS0

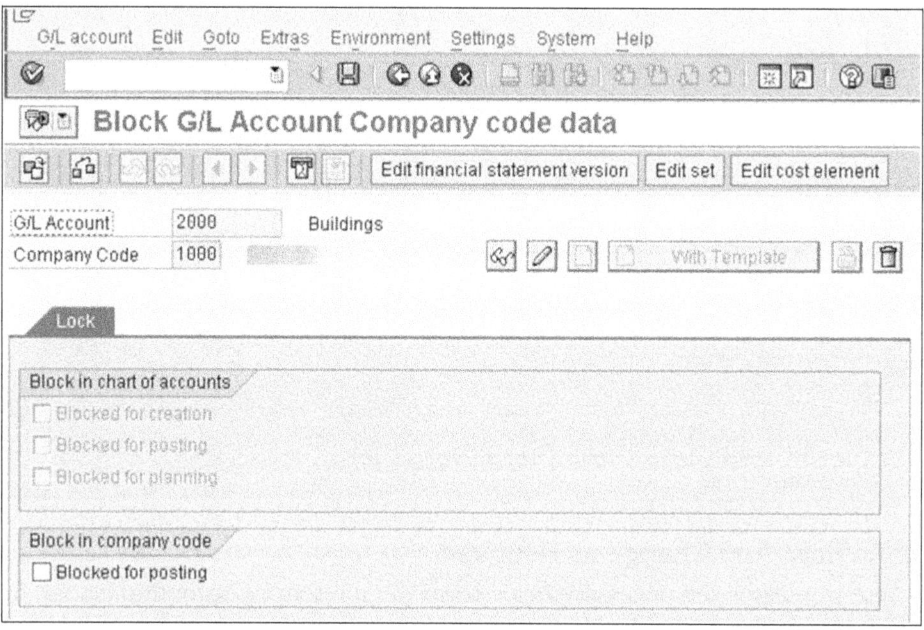

TCode FS00

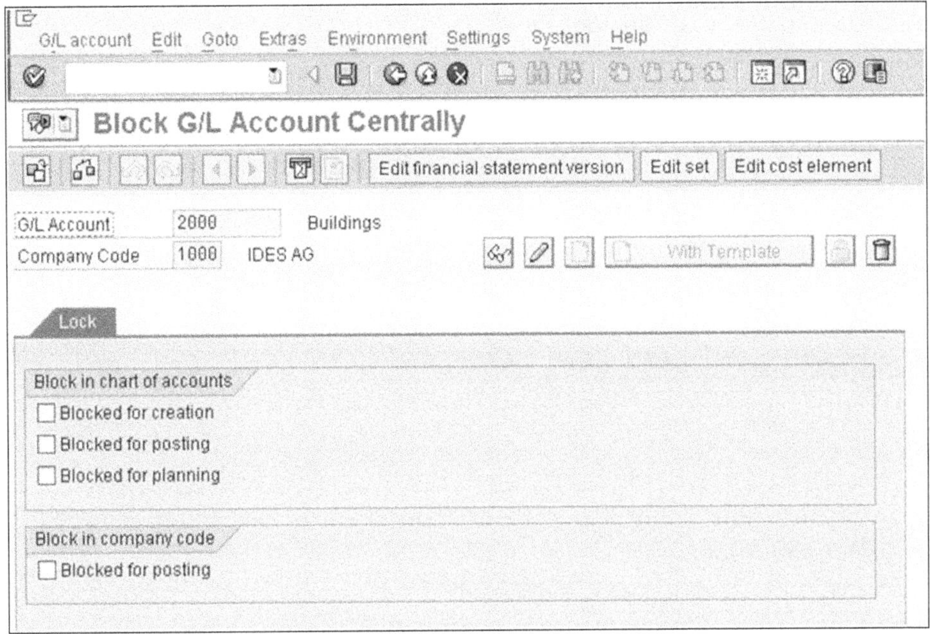

We can create a **posting block** for a GL account using the TCodes FS00 & FSS0. Besides, using the TCode FS00, we can **block an account from being created** in the company codes.

Why should we block an account?

We may come across a business scenario to stop using a particular GL account.

For instance, we have to change the tax category for an account. But the system won't allow that change. We can create a new account with the desired tax category and block postings to the old account in this scenario.

6. Tax Settings in GL Accounts

One of the vital parameters that affect our daily work life is the tax settings in the system. Correct tax settings significantly reduce the chances of errors creeping into the system records.

Let's learn the GL accounts tax settings to maintain them in the correct form.

i) Tax Relevant Accounts

Certain types of accounts are VAT tax-relevant, either input or output tax.

We can broadly list out tax-relevant accounts as:

1) Procurement & expense accounts with input tax, and
2) Sales account with output tax

FSS0 - Edit GL Account in Company Code

Control Data Tab >> Tax Category Field

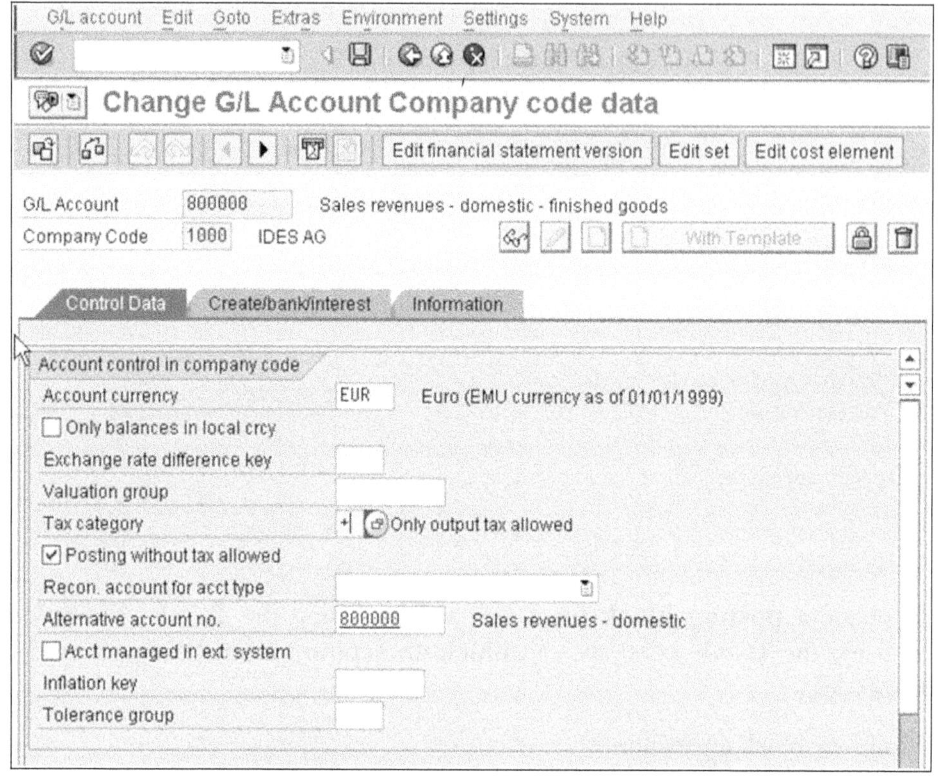

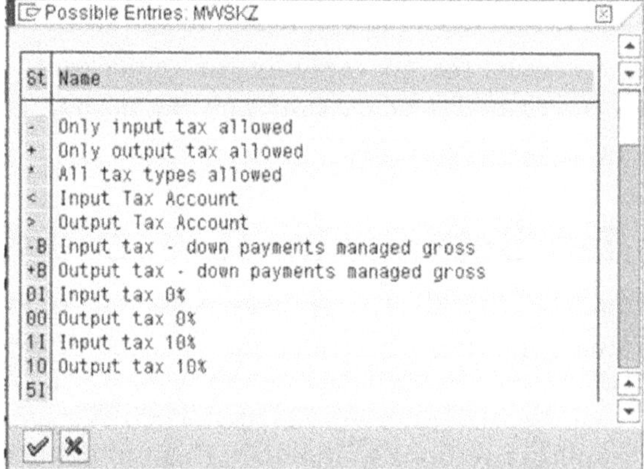

We have the options:

- ✓ **Choose '-' for o**nly input tax allowed
- ✓ **Choose '+' for** only output tax allowed
- ✓ **Choose * for** all tax types allowed

Additionally, there is a check-box 'Posting without Tax Allowed.' Enabling this indicator *allows entries* without tax. However, if we post an entry with tax, the system checks with the input or output tax category defined for that account.

Thus, we need to enable the 'posting without tax allowed' check-box if we have to post 'with tax' and 'without tax' transactions.

The Limitation

We can't do any tax category change to a running account.

If we have to change the tax category to a tax-relevant account, we need to create a new account with the appropriate tax settings and start posting to that new account. Also, we need to block postings to the old account

ii) Tax Accounts

We have seen how to set up *tax-relevant* accounts such as sales accounts, purchase accounts, and expense accounts.

Now, we will learn about *tax accounts.*

Tax accounts are exclusively for posting taxes.

Tax account examples: VAT input tax accounts, VAT output tax accounts.

We can define tax accounts using:

1) '<' Less than sign in the tax category field for **input tax account**
2) '>' Greater than sign in the tax category field for o**utput tax account**

∞

7. Bank Accounts

We need three GL accounts for every bank account in the SAP System: two sub-accounts and one main account.

Sub-Accounts

We need **two bank sub-accounts**: a bank receipts sub-account for posting deposit entries and bank payments sub-account for posting payment entries.

Main Bank Account

In addition to the sub-accounts, we need **one main account**. During the bank reconciliation, transactions posted in the sub-accounts are cleared and posted to the main bank account.

Bank Reconciliation

We enter the bank transactions in either the bank receipts sub-account or the bank payments sub-account as the case may be.

At the time of bank reconciliation,

- ✓ Entries in the bank receipts sub-account are cleared and posted to the main bank account on the 'deposit value date,' and
- ✓ Entries in the bank payments sub-account are cleared and posted to the main bank account when the bank makes the payments.

Thus, when you complete the bank reconciliation,

- ✓ The open items in the bank receipts sub-account is the 'receipts deposited but not yet credited by the bank,'
- ✓ The open items in the bank payments sub-account are the 'payments issued but not cleared in the bank,' and
- ✓ The main bank account balance matches the balance with the bank.

∞

8. GL Accounts List Report

Often, we require the list of GL accounts in the system - either the accounts in a company code or the accounts in the Chart of Accounts.

For example, the GL accounts list helps find a suitable account for entering a particular business transaction.

So, how do we query the system for the list of GL accounts?

i) GL Accounts in the Company Code

S_ALR_87012333 - G/L Accounts List

Using this standard report in the system, we can generate the accounts list for a company code.

The output is a list with a Chart of Account, account code, and account description.

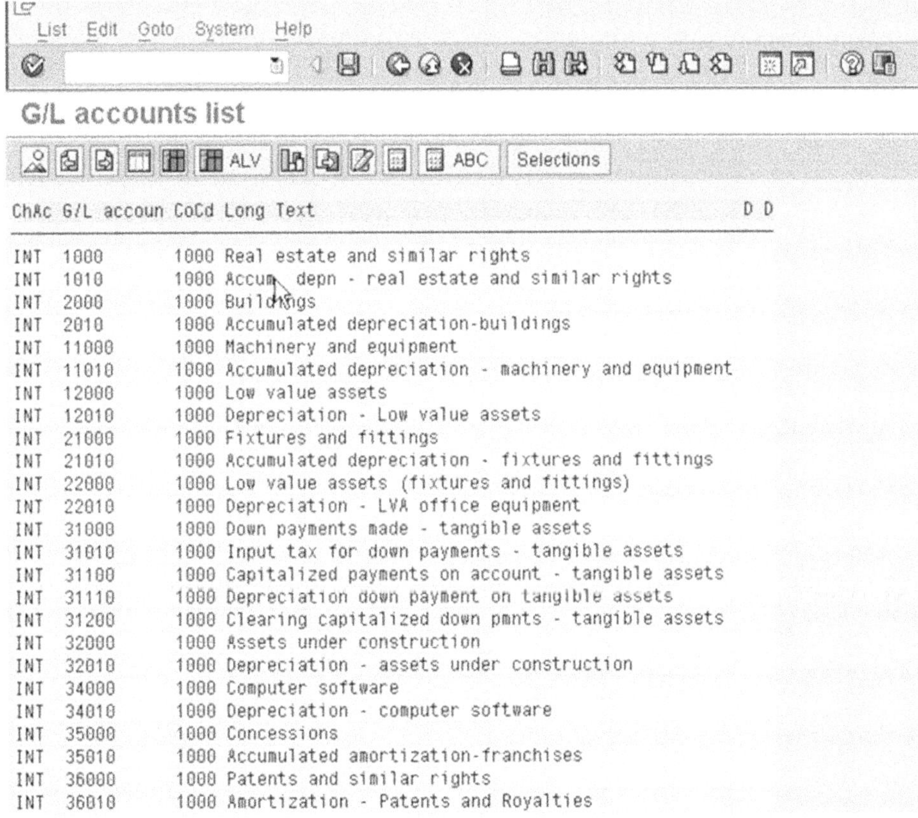

ChAc	G/L accoun	CoCd	Long Text	D	D
INT	1000	1000	Real estate and similar rights		
INT	1010	1000	Accum. depn - real estate and similar rights		
INT	2000	1000	Buildings		
INT	2010	1000	Accumulated depreciation-buildings		
INT	11000	1000	Machinery and equipment		
INT	11010	1000	Accumulated depreciation - machinery and equipment		
INT	12000	1000	Low value assets		
INT	12010	1000	Depreciation - Low value assets		
INT	21000	1000	Fixtures and fittings		
INT	21010	1000	Accumulated depreciation - fixtures and fittings		
INT	22000	1000	Low value assets (fixtures and fittings)		
INT	22010	1000	Depreciation - LVA office equipment		
INT	31000	1000	Down payments made - tangible assets		
INT	31010	1000	Input tax for down payments - tangible assets		
INT	31100	1000	Capitalized payments on account - tangible assets		
INT	31110	1000	Depreciation down payment on tangible assets		
INT	31200	1000	Clearing capitalized down pmnts - tangible assets		
INT	32000	1000	Assets under construction		
INT	32010	1000	Depreciation - assets under construction		
INT	34000	1000	Computer software		
INT	34010	1000	Depreciation - computer software		
INT	35000	1000	Concessions		
INT	35010	1000	Accumulated amortization-franchises		
INT	36000	1000	Patents and similar rights		
INT	36010	1000	Amortization - Patents and Royalties		

ii) GL Accounts in the Chart of Accounts

S_ALR_87012326 - Chart of Accounts

We can get a list report of the accounts in a Chart of Accounts with this report.

The output is a list containing the account codes with account descriptions.

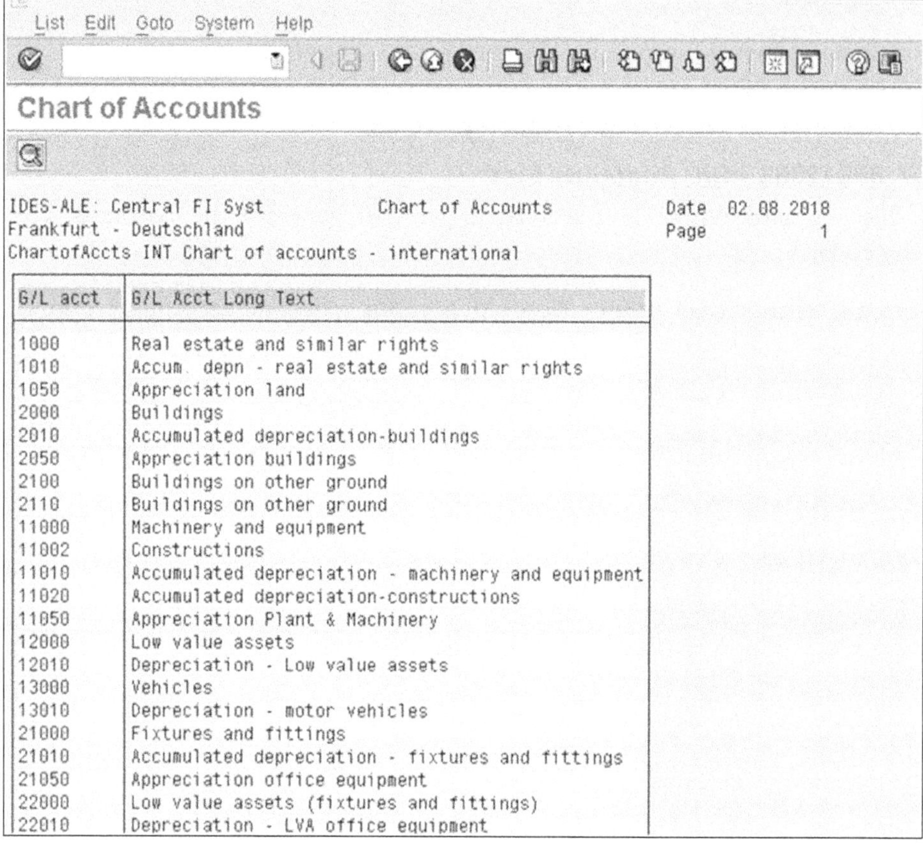

G/L acct	G/L Acct Long Text
1000	Real estate and similar rights
1010	Accum. depn - real estate and similar rights
1050	Appreciation land
2000	Buildings
2010	Accumulated depreciation-buildings
2050	Appreciation buildings
2100	Buildings on other ground
2110	Buildings on other ground
11000	Machinery and equipment
11002	Constructions
11010	Accumulated depreciation - machinery and equipment
11020	Accumulated depreciation-constructions
11050	Appreciation Plant & Machinery
12000	Low value assets
12010	Depreciation - Low value assets
13000	Vehicles
13010	Depreciation - motor vehicles
21000	Fixtures and fittings
21010	Accumulated depreciation - fixtures and fittings
21050	Appreciation office equipment
22000	Low value assets (fixtures and fittings)
22010	Depreciation - LVA office equipment

∞

We have completed the first chapter in the three chapters on master records, learning GL Master Records.

In the next chapter, we'll learn AR & AP Master Records.

∞∞

CHAPTER 3

AR and AP Master Records

We want to maintain the AR & AP masters in the best form because master records control the system working environments such as transaction posting and report generation.

In continuation of learning the financial accounting master records, we will learn in this chapter how to create AR & AP new master records and how to maintain them.

Chapter Contents

1. Creating New Customer /Vendor A/c (With Precaution)
2. Display, Change & Block - Customers & Vendors A/cs
3. All About One-Time Customers /Vendors A/cs, and
4. Creating & Using Worklist

∞

1. Creating New Customer or Vendor Account (With Precaution)

We can create a new customer or a vendor account in three steps.

Step 1: Precaution to Avoid Duplicates

You may have already experienced this scenario if you have handled a group of company codes: duplicate customer or vendor accounts in the system.

Duplicate customer or vendor accounts in the system would pose a problem when extracting reports on customers' or vendors' accounts at the **Group Level.**

We can avoid duplicate account creation by merely searching through the VAT registration code before you proceed to create a new account for a customer or vendor.

Query the system by customer VAT registration number:
S_ALR_87012172 Customer Balances: Dynamic Selections >> Customer Master >> VAT Registration no.

We have the VAT Registration number, and we want to know if any customer account matches the specific VAT /GST number.

It is an excellent test to avoid customer account duplication when we create a new customer account.

Please refer to 'Report by Customer VAT Registration Number' under Chapter 8 Account Balances, Account Statements (page no. 90.)

Step 2: Choose a Reference Account

We have to choose an existing customer or vendor account as the reference account for creating a new customer or vendor account.

Choose the reference account belonging to the same account group.

Account group is the classification & grouping of similar customers or vendors' accounts.

The account group concept is easy to understand with examples.

Examples of account groups:

- ✓ Trade Receivable - Domestic
- ✓ Trade Receivable - Foreign, and
- ✓ One Time Accounts

As an illustration, to create a new domestic customer, choose an existing domestics customer account as a reference account.

Step 3: Create the Account in Company Code

FD01 - Create Customer A/c

FK01 - Create Vendor A/c

The system populates values from the referenced account other than the name, address, and contact details in the new account creation screens.

We can choose to accept the defaulted values or change them as required before saving the master record.

Use the TCode FD01 /FK01, provide a reference account, enter the name and contact details and review the master data values defaulted from the referenced account and press the **save** button to complete the creation of a new account.

∞

2. Display, Change & Block the Customers' & Vendors' Accounts

i) Display Accounts Data

FD03 - Display Customer A/c

FK03 - Display Vendor A/c

There are three sets of data associated with the customers' and the vendors' masters.

a) General Data: Name, Address & Contact Details. General data is common to and is shared by all the company codes in the system.

b) Company Code Data: Payment terms and dunning procedure. These are company code specific. Each company code should create this data as per their agreement with the customer or the vendor.

c) Sales Area /Purchasing Organization Data: The sales department creates the sales order data for the customer accounts. The purchasing department enters and maintains the purchase order data for the vendor accounts.

ii) Change Customer or Vendor Account

FD02 - Change Customer Account

FK02 - Change Vendor Account

Often, you have to change or update customer or vendor master records.

There may be changes in address or contact person details; you may have to change the payment terms or the dunning procedure.

Only persons in your department having adequate system authorization can make the required changes.

iii) Blocking Customer or Vendor Account

A series of transactions occur in a customer account: sales order, goods delivery, invoicing, dunning, and payment collection.

Similarly, vendor account transactions include purchase orders, invoice receipts, payments for the purchases, etc.

We may have to block a customer's or a vendor's accounts for specific transactions. Thus, the system has the following block options:

i) Customer A/c Sales Block
ii) Vendor A/c Purchasing Block
iii) Vendor A/c Payment Block
iv) Customer /Vendor: Posting Block, and

v) Customer A/c Dunning Block

a) Customer Account Sales Block

XD05 - Block /Unblock

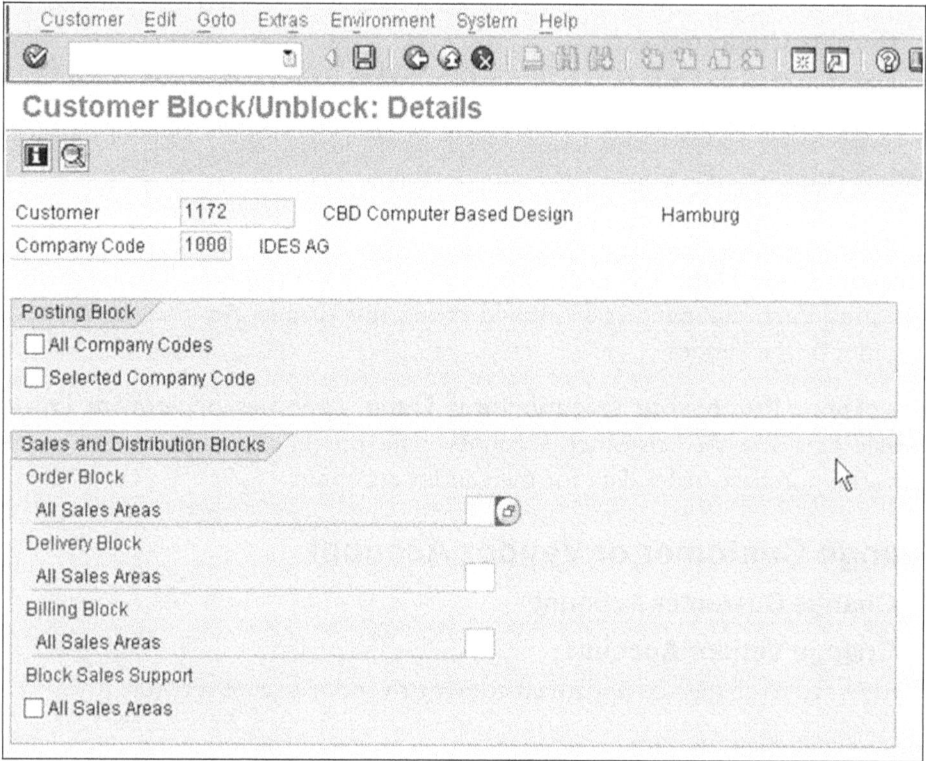

Order block is the most likely restriction we want to put on a customer account. When we place a customer account under the 'order block,' the sales team cannot enter new orders.

Depending on the system authorization matrix, customer order blocking may be vested with the sales team.

b) Vendor Account Purchasing Block

XK05 - Block/Unblock

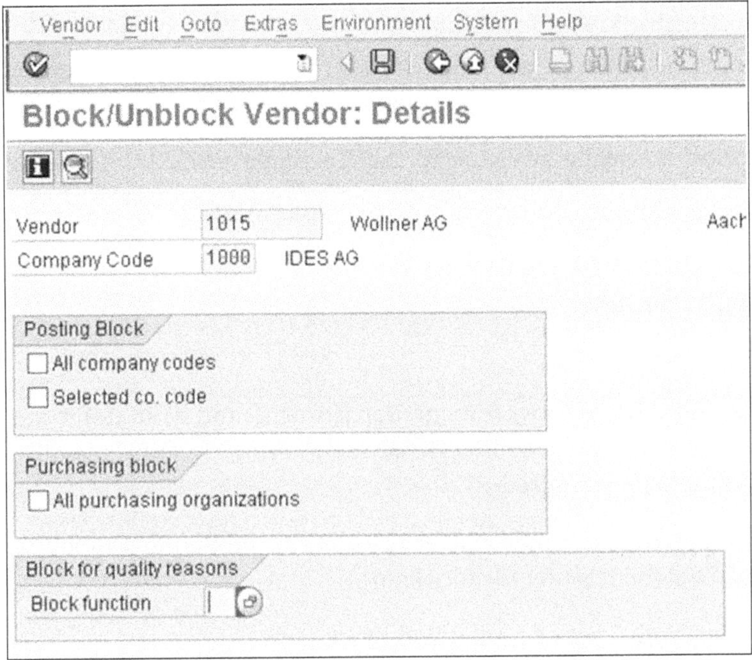

We can block a vendor account for the purchase transactions using the TCode XK05.

c) Vendor Account Payment Block

Master Records >> Change

Choose: Payment Transactions

You need to change the master record for the payments block:

Block Key

We need to enter a 'block key' in the vendor master record— **payment block field.** These keys represent reasons for blocking.

Block Key examples:

Block Indicator	Description
(blank)	Free for payment
*	Skip Account
A	Blocked for payment
R	Invoice verification

d) Customer or Vendor: Posting Block

FD05 - Block /Unblock Customer A/c

FK05 - Block /Unblock Vendor A/c

Before blocking a customer or a vendor account for the posting transactions, make sure there are no open items. Otherwise, we won't be able to clear them.

This authorization is usually available to the Accounts team. Using these TCodes, you can block posting transactions to a customer or a vendor account.

e) Customer Account Dunning Block

FD02 - Customer Change

Choose: Correspondence

Your customer may be a Government department, and you don't want to send a payment reminder from the accounts department. Also, in some countries, by custom, no customer follow-up is required.

You need to change the customer master records for the dunning block. Use 'block key' - the key that shows the reasons for blocking.

The system comes with a set of predefined block keys.

For example, block key 'A' means, **'Manual block due to a telephone payment advice.'**

∞

3. One-Time Customers and Vendors Account

The system provides for one-time accounts creation that facilitates hassle-free follow-ups and correspondence.

We enter the customer-specific information like name, address, and bank details in the transaction document in a one-time account. During the transaction posting, the system automatically goes to a screen for entering the name, address, bank details, etc.

You can dun open items using the dunning program and pay using the automatic payment program for the one-time accounts.

Sort Key 022: Customer Name, City

Sort keys in the master record populate selected data in the 'assignment field' when you post a transaction in the system.

Use the **Sort Key '022'** in the one-time account master record to populate **Customer Name & City** in the 'assignment fields' of the line items.

Sort key '022' in the one-time master record enables the system to sort your transaction records of one-time customers and vendors in the order of 'Name & City.'

Line items sorted by customer name & city are helpful when we run the dunning program and the payment program.

∞

We have learned how to create & and maintain customers' & vendors' accounts.

The next chapter, AR & AP Master Records' Key Parameters, is the last in the three-chapter financial accounting master records lessons.

Please continue reading.

∞∞

CHAPTER 4

AR & AP Master Record Key Parameters

We carry out multiple tasks such as dunning, automatic payments, generating statements of accounts in AR & AP sub-ledgers. We need to keep the master record parameters in the correct format for best results in system tasks.

Let us learn what those key parameters are and how to keep them in the correct format.

Chapter Contents

∞

1. Payment Terms

The system generates the outstanding or overdue items list, due date analysis, and payment forecast reports by referring to the payment terms. Thus, the payment terms are essential to control receivable follow-ups and timely payments to vendors.

Let's now refer to the payment terms that come predefined with the SAP system:

Pay. term	Description
0001	Payable immediately Due net
0002	Within 14 days 3 % cash discount
	Within 30 days 2 % cash discount
	Within 45 days Due net

We may have different business scenarios requiring additional payment terms. This is a technical task; we need to take the system support team's help to create new terms in the system.

i) Changing the Payment Terms

FD02 - Change Customer Account

Button: Company Code Tab: Payment Transactions

FK02 - Change Vendor Account

Select: Payment Transactions check-box: Company code data

We need to create the payment terms as agreed with the customers or the vendors if it is not already defined.

Then, we can update the payment terms code in the 'terms of payment' field.

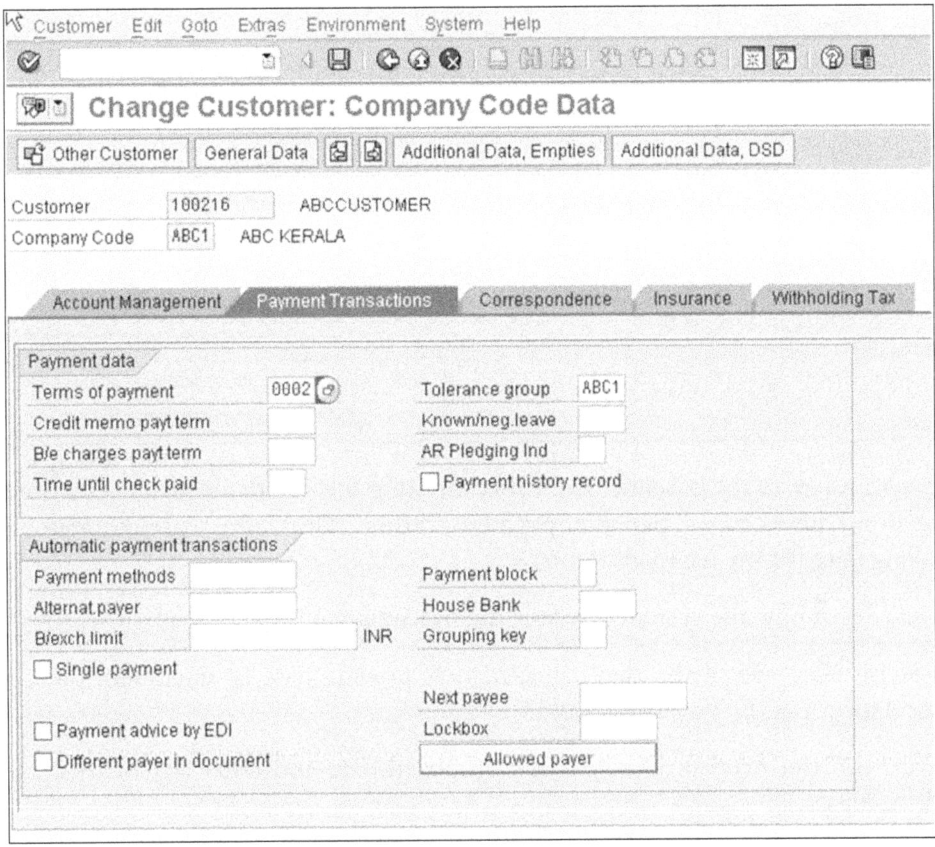

The master data payment terms apply to the entire customer's or the vendor's transactions. However, this is subject to an exception; the system will ignore the master data payment term when we enter a different payment term for a particular invoice.

ii) Baseline Date

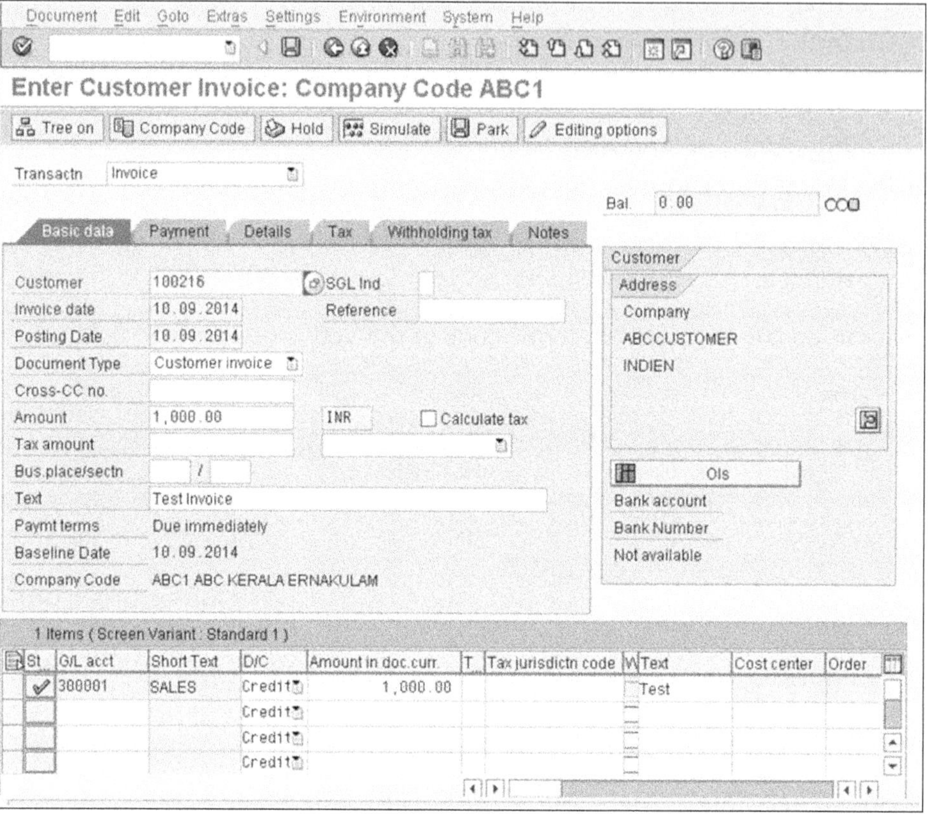

The system refers to the baseline date for computing the due dates for the customers' or the vendors' invoices as per the payment terms. Thus, the baseline date is the controlling date for the payment terms.

Now, let's learn how the system captures the baseline date.

The system takes one of the two dates, namely posting date or document date, as the baseline date as per the configuration.

However, you can override the system's proposed date and enter any other date for a specific invoice.

As an example, consider posting a vendor invoice for the purchase of a piece of machinery. As per your manager's advice, you want to calculate the payment term from the day installation is complete.

In this scenario, you can override the system's proposed date and enter the machinery installation date as the baseline date.

∞

2. Dunning Procedure

The dunning procedure is the customers' outstanding collection follow-up procedure.

Sales collection automation is possible by maintaining the dunning procedure in the customers' master records.

Receivable follow-up using a system-defined dunning procedure enables a systematic approach for collecting outstanding dues.

i) Dunning Implementation

FD02 - Customer Change

Company Code Data - Correspondence

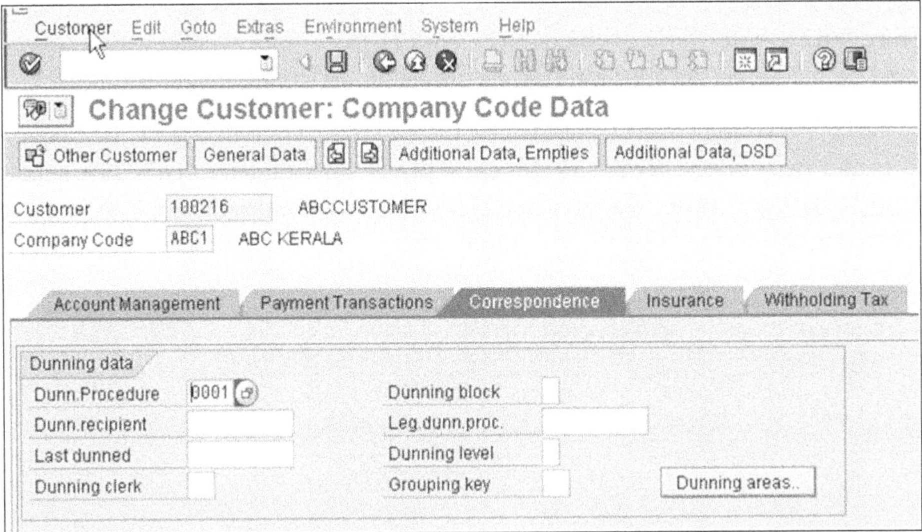

a) Dunning Procedures Configuration

The dunning procedure consists of *dunning levels* and *dunning forms.*

Dunning levels refer to the number of follow-up correspondence and the interval between the follow-ups.

Example: Four-level dunning, every two weeks.

Dunning forms are the reminder letter formats. The severity of the reminder letters escalates with each level, from first correspondence to second, and so on. Dunning forms are predefined and configured for each dunning level.

SAP comes with predefined dunning levels and forms. We can modify the predefined dunning levels and forms to suit our business scenario with the system support team's help.

b) Assign Dunning Procedure to Customer Master Record

We need to assign a dunning procedure in the customer master record whose receivable dunning is required using the TCode FD02.

c) Run Dunning Program

F150 - Dunning

The dunning program is similar to the automatic payment program with 'run on date & run identification.'

The dunning program is run periodically for sending out payment reminders.

∞

3. Assigning AR & AP Accounts to Accounting Clerks

We communicate with the customers and vendors from time to time. We send out the statement of accounts, outstanding statements, dunning letters, and so on.

We can have the system print the name of the accounting clerk who is responsible for that customer or vendor account in the communications that we send. The accounting clerk's name makes it easier for the customers and vendors to get any clarification they need regarding the contents of the communications sent to them.

The TCodes

FD02 - Customer Change

Company Code Area >> Correspondence: Acctg Clerk field

FK02 - Vendor Change

Company Code data - Correspondence: Acctg Clerk field

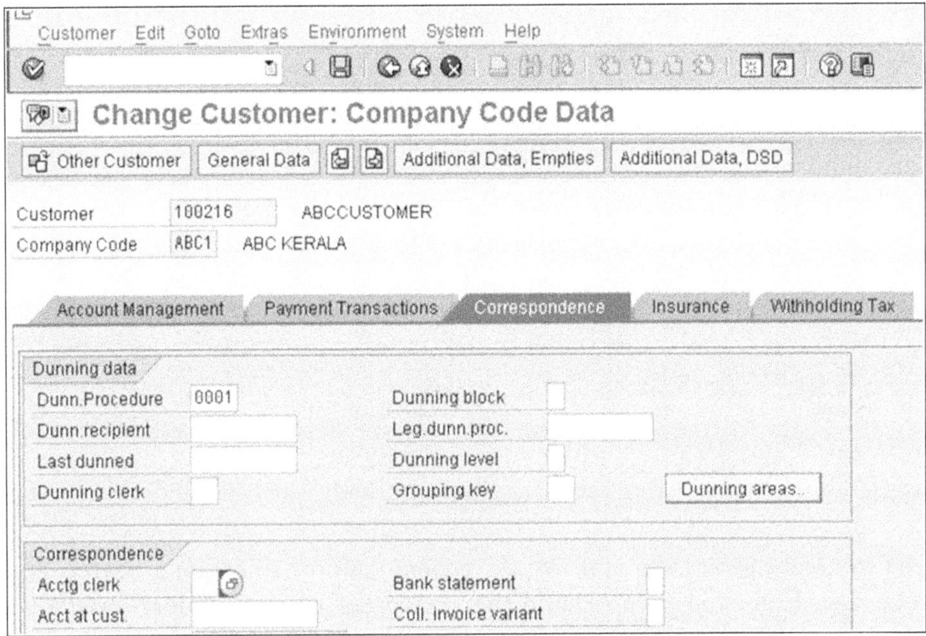

First, the system support team should create 'user IDs' for the Accounting Clerks.

Then, we can update the 'Accounting Clerk user id' in the customers' and the vendors' master records, Correspondence: Acctg Clerk field using the TCodes: FD02 and FK02.

∞

4. Defining Corporate Groups

It is often the case two or more customers or vendors belong to a business group.

In that scenario, it is helpful if the system identifies those customers or vendors as belonging to a 'group' to enable us to analyze the group of customers' or the vendors' accounts together.

Corporate group-wise account analysis is possible by entering a user-defined key in the 'corporate group' field.

The TCodes

FD02 - Customer Change

General Data -> Control -> Corporate Group

FK02 - Vendor Change

General Data -> Control -> Corporate Group

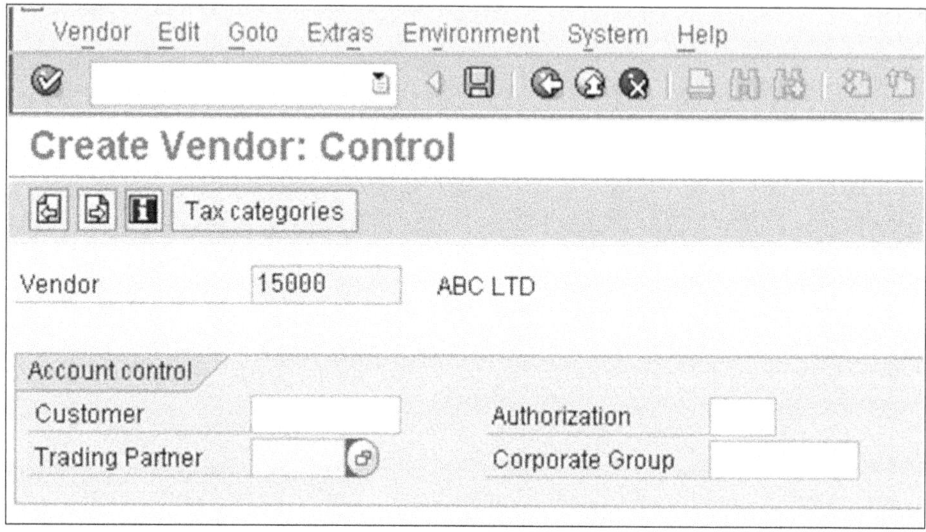

We need to coin a group key and request system support to create a **match code** for the group key. Enter the group key in the customers' or the vendors' master records that belong to a group.

Now, we can generate reports for the group.

Let's explain the group key's benefits with an example.

FBL5N Customer Line Item Display: Dynamic Selection

Consider, we have identified three customers ABC Trading Ltd, ABC Contracting Company, and ABC Clothing, as belonging to a business group.

The system support team has to create the mach code for 'ABC Group' in the system.

We need to input the 'corporate group' field of the selected customer master records, the group key - ABC Group.

We can now generate a combined system report FBL5N for the three companies by selecting ABC Group in the **'dynamic selection.'**

Please refer to Report by Customer Business Group (page no. 89) under Chapter 8 Account Balances, Account Statements to learn how to create this report using dynamic selections.

∞

5. How to Sort Line Items (and Its Benefits)

When you query the system for a Statement of Account, the system generates the statement with line items presented in particular sort order.

In the system, we can control the line item sorting.

What are the benefits of sorting the line item in a particular order?

We'll learn that now.

i) Sort Order and Its Benefits

We know that the purchase order number is the common field that connects the receipt of goods entries and the vendor invoice entries in the GR/IR account.

Therefore, it's good to have the statement of account of GR/IR account with the line items sorted by a purchase order number, correct?

Similarly, we can have line items sorting for vendors' account statements by vendor invoice numbers and line items sorting for one-time customers or vendors' account statements by 'Customer /Vendor Name & City.'

We understand the benefits of a particular line items sort order.

Let's now learn how to get this done in the system.

ii) Assignment Number Field

Assignment number is a line item field. Assignment number controls how the transaction records are sorted and presented in the reports.

When we extract a report of transactions for the GL, customer, or vendor accounts, the system defaults the line items by the 'assignment number field' content.

Now, there is a way to control the assignment number field content.

This is possible using the 'sort key' in the master record.

iii) Sort Keys

The sort key is a three-digit numerical number. Sort keys in the master records enable the system to default the assignment number field content during the data entry.

In other words, the master record sort key determines how the system populates the assignment field when we post a transaction in the system.

The system comes with a set of predefined sort keys.

The sort keys and the data that get populated are:

Sort Key	Description
000	Assignment Number Field will be left blank
001	Posting Date
009	Vendor Invoice no.
014	Purchase Order no.

Examples where the sort keys are helpful:

a) GR/IR Account - Sort Key '014'

GR/IR account statement with line items sorted by purchase order number is possible with sort key 014 in the GR/IR account master record.

Sort key 014 in the GR/IR Account master record enables the system to automatically populate the assignment number fields with purchase order numbers during the receipt of goods and vendor invoice postings in the system.

Purchase order numbers in the assignment fields of GR/IR account entries make it easier to identify the vendor invoices entries and the corresponding goods receipt entries together for clearing.

b) Vendors Accounts - Sort Key '009'

Sort key '009' in the vendor master enables vendor invoice no. to populate the assignment number fields of invoices posted.

The vendor invoice number in the assignment field enables the system to clear off invoices vs. payment entries in the vendor accounts.

c) One-time Customer and Vendor Accounts - Sort Key '022.'

The one-time customers' account master record has the sort key '022'. The sort key 022 populates the assignment field with 'Customer Name, City' during the one-time account transactions postings.

We understand the benefits of sort keys. Let us learn the TCodes for setting the sort keys.

iv) The TCodes

FD02 - Change Customer Master Record

Company Code Data: Account Management Tab >> Accounting Information >> Sort Key

FK02 - Change Vendor Master Record

Company Code Data: Accounting Information >> Sort Key

FSS0 Edit GL Account

Control Data Tab: Sort Key

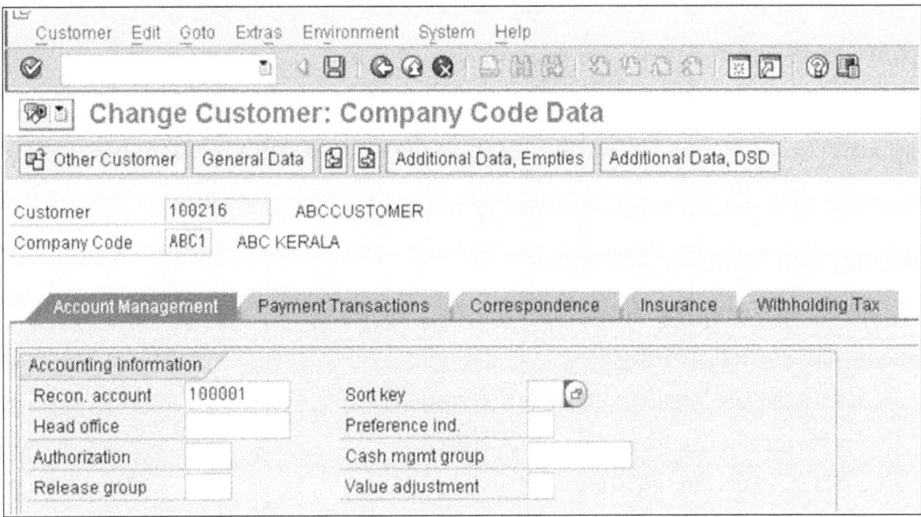

∞

We've completed the financial accounting master records lessons. In the next chapter, we will learn Document Posting TCodes.

∞∞

CHAPTER 5

Document Posting TCodes

We know data is captured in the GL, AR & AP by manual entries and interfacing entries from other modules.

For manual transaction entries, we need to use TCodes.

We will learn the **best ones among the various TCodes**, the unique features of these TCodes, and the scenarios we can use them to derive maximum productivity.

Chapter Contents

1. Posting Simple Entries in GL
2. Posting Complex Entries in GL
3. Cash Journal Postings
4. Customer & Vendor Invoice Postings
5. Customer & Vendor Payments Entry
6. GR/IR Account Posting
7. Automatic Postings
8. Printing Vouchers

1. Posting Simple Entries in GL

We know some entries are simple, just two or three line items. In this topic, we will learn the TCodes for posting such simple transactions in the GL.

The TCodes

F-02 - General Posting

F-65 - General Document Parking

We can post to both *GL and Customer or Vendor Accounts*. We have to use posting keys and a reference document. Also, we can hold the document or open a held document for further correction & post.

We can select the 'Fast Data Entry' button to go to the fast entry screen when we have multiple GL Line items to enter.

We cannot park a document using this TCode F-02. To park, we have to use TCode F-65 - General Document Parking.

Simple Entry Scenarios

1. Entry for rent expense:

Rent A/c (GL)	Dr
Landlord A/c (AP)	Cr

2. Adjustment or correction entries.

Using the Account Assignment Model

The account assignment model is a data entry template.

For repetitive kind of GL document entries in the system, we can create account assignment models to reduce the manual work and minimize posting errors.

Please refer to the Account Assignment Template (page no. 45) later in this chapter to learn how to create and use this template.

∞

2. Posting Complex Entries in GL

Often, we have to enter GL entries with multiple line items. Such entries are usually posted by Accountants well versed with debit and credit.

The TCode

FB50 - Enter G/L Account Document

We don't need the posting keys when we use the TCode FB50.

Using FB50, we can post complex GL entries - entries with multiple line items.

We can post with a reference document. If we have a similar entry already in the system, we can use that entry as a reference document.

When we cannot complete the entry in one go for any reason, we can hold the document to complete and post it later. Later we can recall a **held** document to complete the entry and post as we get the required additional information.

Also, we can park the document that we can post later.

Scenarios Where TCode FB50 Can be Used

1) Insurance Expense
2) Utility Payments
3) GL Rectification Entries

∞

3. Cash Journal Postings

Cash Journal Posting is a petty cash transaction posting TCode. Each petty cash accountant can have their cash journal in the system for data entry and control their petty cash.

For example, consider a company having three site offices with a petty cashier at each site. In this scenario, we can create separate cash journals in the system under the responsibility of the site petty cashiers.

The TCode

FBCJ - Cash Journal Posting

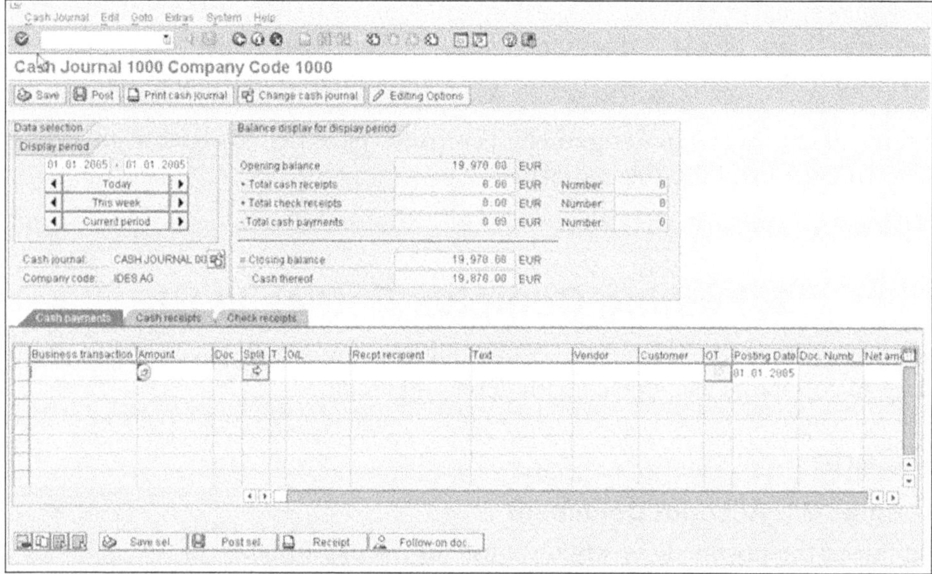

Advantages of Cash Journal Posting

- ✓ We can post cash receipts and payment transactions on a single screen.
- ✓ We have access to daily, weekly or current period on-screen cash status reports.
- ✓ Daily cash position, including opening balance, total receipts, total payments, and closing balance, is automatically calculated and displayed by the system.
- ✓ Printing a cash journal is easy.
- ✓ A two-step procedure of saving then post later at day-end helps avoid mistakes.

Besides, the cash journal prevents negative cash balance.

∞

4. Customer & Vendor Invoice Postings

There are two invoice types in the system:

i) Invoices raised in SD and MM modules, and

ii) Invoices raised in the FI module.

i) SD & MM Module Invoices

SD Module Customer Invoices: The sales department creates customer invoices in the Sales & Distribution module.

SD module invoices interface with GL automatically as per the system configuration.

MM Module Vendor Invoices: The accounts department enters the vendor invoices using the TCode MIRO, a *Materials Management Module TCode.*

We will discuss invoice postings using the TCode MIRO later in this chapter under GR/IR Account Postings topic.

ii) FI Invoices

FB70 - Customer Invoice

FB60 - Vendor Invoice

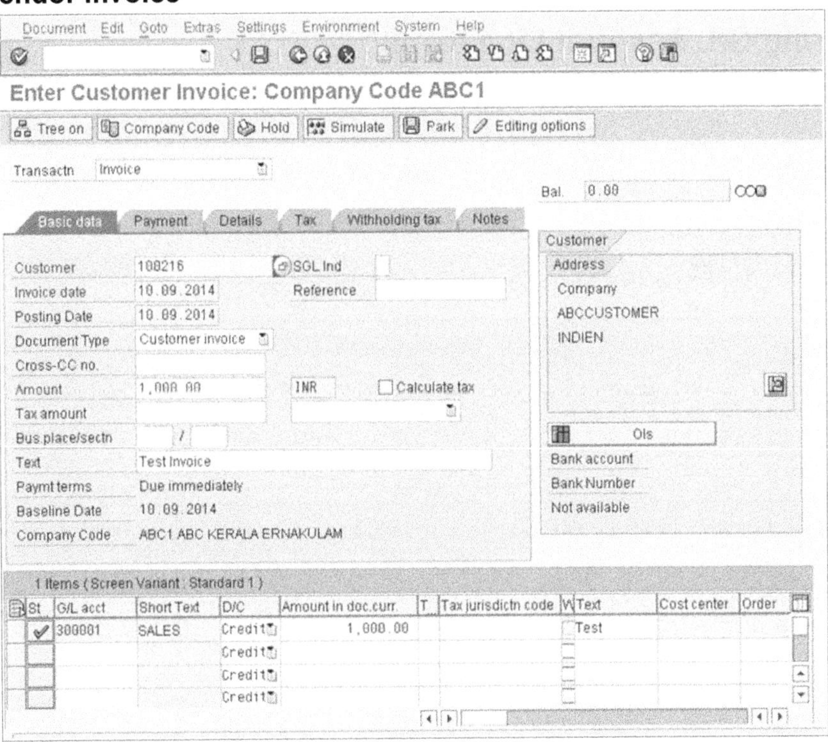

The TCodes, FB70 & FB60 are for customer and vendor invoice entries in AR & AP sub-ledgers.

The question is, why are there invoice entry options in AR & AP?

The reasoning behind AR & AP invoice entry options is straightforward. AR & AP invoice entry options are helpful to enter customers' and vendors' invoices that do not have sales orders or purchase orders associated with them in the system.

Let's make it simpler with narrations.

Consider a stationery purchase. We do not create a purchase order in the MM Module for the office stationery purchase in most circumstances. We can post this purchase invoice via AP sub-ledger TCode, FB60 - Vendor Invoice Entry.

Similarly, consider selling an old printer in our office on credit terms. We can post this transaction using the AR TCode FB70 - Invoice Entry.

Having understood why we post invoices in AR /AP modules, let us learn the TCodes' features.

Both the TCodes FB70 & FB60 have very similar design & functionalities.

- ✓ We can hold, open a held doc, and delete a held document.
- ✓ We can park, select parked doc, delete a parked document
- ✓ We can post with a reference document.
- ✓ We can use account assignment templates.

a) Entering G/L Account Line Items

Sales Account Code

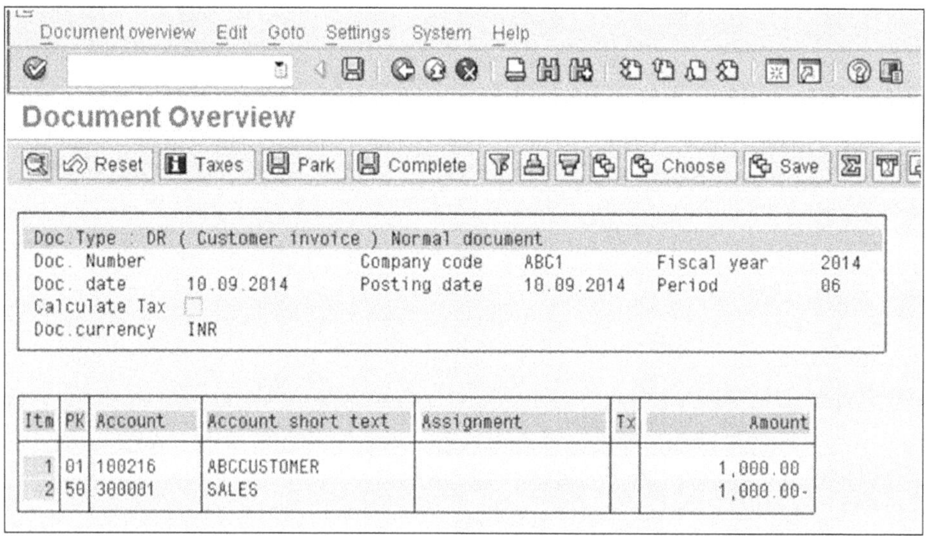

Invoice entry requires a GL line item for the sales account.

Take care to choose the correct sales account code. Choose the sales account that is different from the sales account used for posting SD module sales.

Select GL sales account code, select credit, enter amount & tax code, and choose a cost center or an internal order.

The cost center is optional, as this line item is a revenue entry.

Purchase Account Code

Similar to FI sales, choose the correct purchase account code. Choose the purchase account code different from the one used to post MM module purchases.

b) Account Assignment Template

Main Menu: Account Assignment Template >> Save Account Assignment Template

AAT is a data entry template. When we have a repetition of an invoice posting, we can create an account assignment template and make the invoice posting task much easier to execute.

Create an invoice. Check if everything is okay by clicking 'simulate' and again review the entry one more time. When you are satisfied with the entry, go back to the previous screen, and choose:

> Main menu: Account Assignment Template >> Save Account Assignment Template.

Give a name to the template which you can remember.

Next time when you create an invoice, in the initial screen FB70, enter the customer number, invoice date, and the posting date. Click the **'Tree on'** button to view the account assignment templates. Choose your 'template' and double click to get the GL Account fields filled.

You have to enter the amount and text fields.

Account assignment templates make the invoice posting error-free.

c) Invoice Specific Payment Terms

Payment tab: We can enter invoice-specific payment terms. Invoice-specific payment terms override the master record payment terms.

Usually, the payment terms defined in the customer or the vendor master records are applicable for the SD module and MM module invoices. For FI invoices, we may need a different payment term. We can use the 'payment tab' fields during invoice entry for entering the invoice-specific payment terms.

d) Invoice Specific Payment Block

Payment tab - Payment Block field: We can block payment for an invoice item for a vendor using block keys. Examples of block keys include 'Blocked for payment,' 'Invoice Verification,' and the like.

The default block key is **'Free for payment.'**

Based on the block key we choose, the system allows or blocks the payment for that vendor invoice.

Please refer to Blocking Customer or Vendor Account (page no. 25) under Chapter 3 AR and AP Master Records for other types of blocking AR & AP accounts.

∞

5. Customer & Vendor Payments Entry

i) Receipts from Customers

F-28 - Incoming Payments

We can use the TCode F-28 for accounting for the receipts from the customers.

We can post the receipt and close the open invoices using the button 'process open items.'

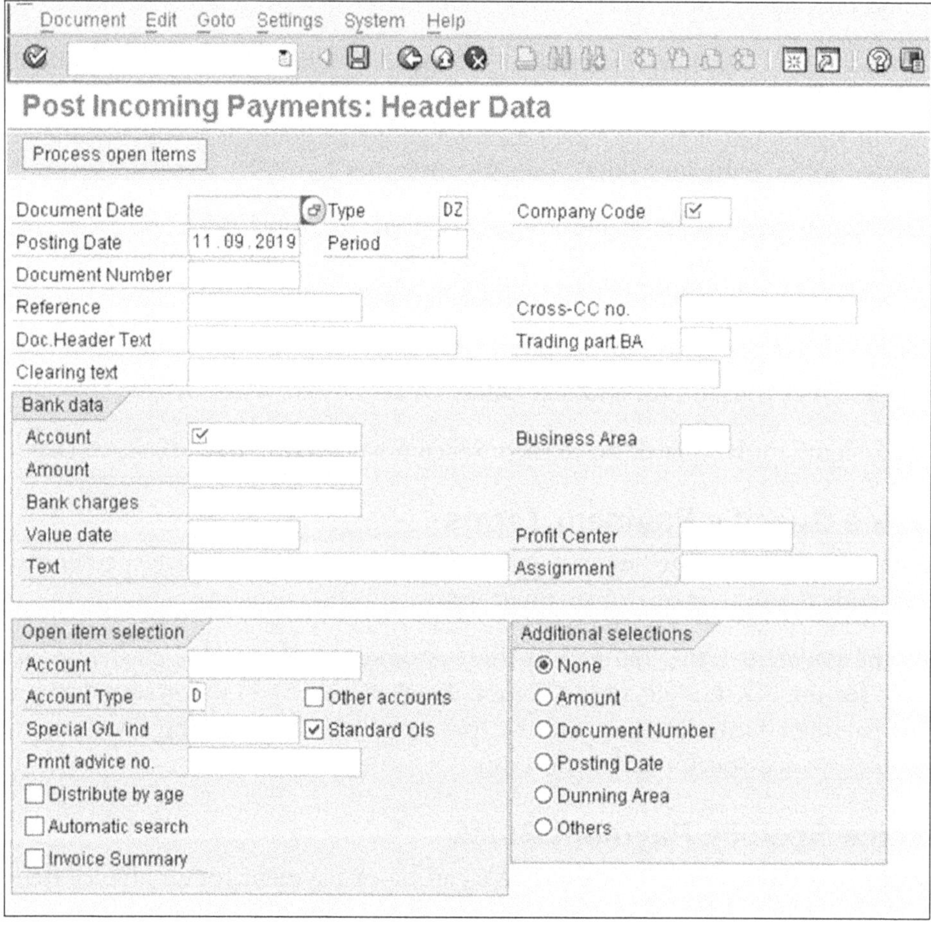

ii) Manual Payments to Vendors

a) With Check Number Control

F-58 - Post + Print Forms

F-58 is the TCode for check payments posting with check lot control.

Let me explain a check lot control just in case you're not aware of it already. We can control the checks by maintaining check lots in the system. We need to enter the beginning and ending numbers of the checks we receive from the bank.

The system controls and allots the check numbers for payment entries using the TCode F-58. We can make a payment entry and print the check.

Also, we can select the vendor invoices and clear them.

b) Without Check Number Control

F-53 - Post Outgoing Payment

If we do not maintain the check number control in the system, we can use the TCode F-53 to pay our vendor and print the check using a different software.

iii) Automatic Payments Program

F110 - Payments

The automatic payment program automates vendor payments. The program analyzes the selected vendor accounts for invoices due for payment and releases the payment after review and approval.

We can complete an automatic payment run in 4 steps.

Step 1: Parameter Selection

Select the payment method like 'bank transfer' and the vendors whose invoices you want to pay and save.

Status shows 'Parameters have been entered.'

Step 2: Payment Proposal

The system prepares a payment proposal with the invoices due under each vendor.

Status shows 'Payment Proposal has been created.'

Review the payment proposal by pressing the 'Proposal Log' button and approve.

Step 3: Payment Run

The system makes the payments to the vendor's bank accounts from the house bank in the payment run.

Status shows 'Payment run has been carried out.'

Step 4: Payment Completed

When you complete the payment process, you get the system status similar to:

'Posting Orders: 56 generated, 56 posted.'

Also, the vendor invoices are cleared in the system as paid.

We can check this using the TCode FBL1N Display/Change Line Items

In the automatic payment method, the system clears the vendor invoices included in the payment run.

iv) Partial Payments

F-59 - Payment Request

Partial payments refer to making payment for the part amount of an invoice.

To make a partial payment, we need to create a **payment request** for the actual amount we want to pay.

Payment requests are 'noted items.' Noted items are non-financial entries in the system; they are one-sided or single-line entries. Noted items do not update ledger balances; they are memo entries.

Let us understand the partial payment with an example.

Consider, we want to pay $ 5,000 against a vendor invoice for $ 10,000. We create a payment request for $ 5,000 using the TCode F-59.

The system blocks the vendor invoice, and only the payment request is available for payment. We can run the payment program to pay the payment request.

v) Payments for Parked Invoices

Consider, we want to release payment towards a parked vendor invoice. We can release the payment by creating a payment request for the parked invoice using the TCode 'F-59 - Payment Request' and running the payment program.

vi) Posting Partial Payments

The payment against a customer invoice is not matching with the invoice amount; there is a difference. When the difference is negligible, we choose to write-off.

However, if the difference between the payment and the invoice is not small, we have two options to account for that payment transaction:

a) Partial Payment, and
b) Residual Payment.

a) Partial Payments

When we choose the partial payment option, the system keeps both the invoice and the payment against that invoice as open items.

The system records the relationship between the two entries: invoice and payment by inserting the invoice reference in the payment entry.

b) Residual Items

If we use the residual items option to post a partial payment, the system closes the invoice and posts the difference amount as a new item.

Which one is the best?

Both choices are right; you can use either of them.

However, use any one of the options consistently and avoid confusion for your colleagues handling the payables and customers when they receive an account statement.

∞

6. GR/IR Account Posting

The acronym GR/IR stands for goods receipt, invoice receipt. GR/IR account is a transitory account between the two modules: Materials Management and the GL.

We post the receipt of goods and the vendor invoices in the GR/IR account.

i) Goods Receipt Entry

MIGO - Goods Movement

Stores department enters the receipt of the goods in the system.

The journal entry is:

Raw Materials Inventory A/c	Dr
GR/IR Account	Cr

ii) Vendor Invoice Entry

MIRO - Enter Invoice

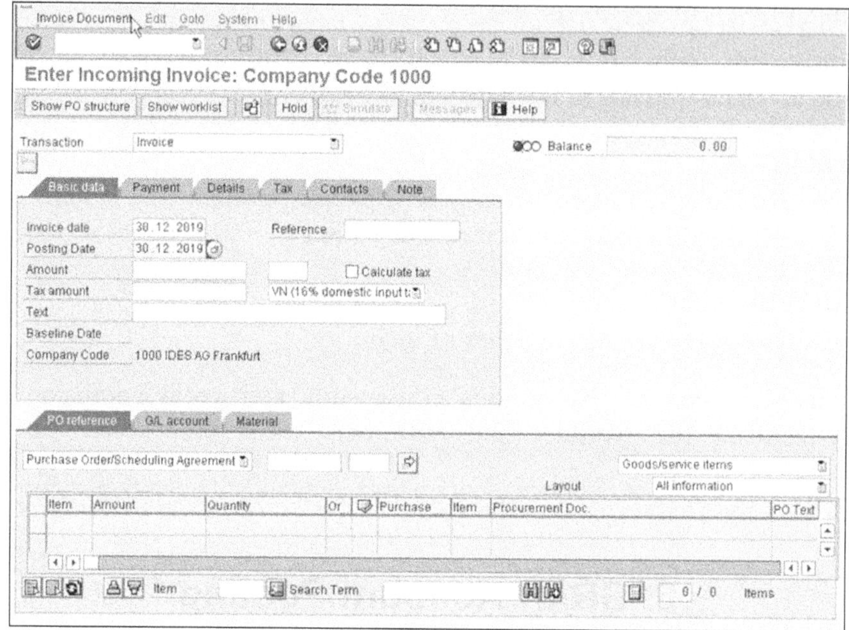

The Accounts department enters the vendor invoice in the system using the TCode MIRO.

The journal entry is:

GR/IR account	Dr
Vendor's account	Cr

iii) GR/IR Account Clearing

We have goods receipts and vendor invoice entries in the GR/IR account that need clearing. We clear the two entries with purchase order number as the common parameter in a three-way matching.

We will learn GR/IR account clearing (page no. 66) under chapter 7 Document Clearing.

∞

7. Automatic Posting

Automatic posting refers to additional line items generated by the system automatically during a transaction entry. The system is configured to post automated entries in specific transaction entry scenarios.

For example, when posting a receipt from a customer, the system automatically posts a negligible difference amount to an expense account.

We enter into the system the customer receipt and match it with the customer invoice and simulate.

Now, suppose there is a small difference. The system generates an automatic posting line item to write off that difference. It displays the automatic entry and the entries we made for customer account credit and bank account debit in the 'simulate' screen.

The entry so generated by the system is the automatic posting. The system creates automatic postings as per the configuration.

The advantage is clear; it saves time taken for data entry of writing off the small difference & reduces the incidence of error.

We can check the automatic entries through **'simulation'** before posting the transaction in the system.

Scenarios Where We Can Automate

We have four business scenarios for automating the entries. They are:

1) Writing off Small Amount
2) Cash Discount
3) Exchange Rate Difference, and
4) Line Items for Tax

How Does the System Generate Automatic Entries?

The system generates automatic entries for the 1 to 3 above, as per the '**tolerance groups**' configuration. Your system admin team can help you with the tolerance group configuration.

The system generates automatic tax line items per tax category definition in the GL account master data: please refer to Tax Relevant Accounts (page no. 17) under Chapter 2 GL Master Records.

∞

8. Printing Documents

As Accountants, we need supporting documents either in digital form or hard copy for the transactions posted in the system. The supporting documents help understand a transaction and act as evidence during the audit.

We can print the supporting documents in two steps:

Step 1: Create Document Print Requests and

Step 2: Print the Documents from the Requests created in step 1.

Step 1: Creating Document Print Requests

F.62 Internal Documents

We can create document print requests for a range of GL, AR, and AP documents with TCode F.62. The document print request is a system record.

F.62 Internal Documents is a very flexible option, enabling us to create 'print requests' for documents of our choice.

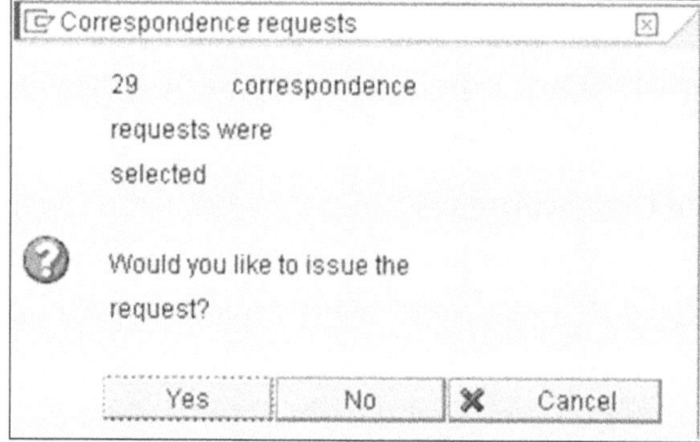

Step 2: Printing Documents from the Requests

F.64 - Maintain Correspondence Requests

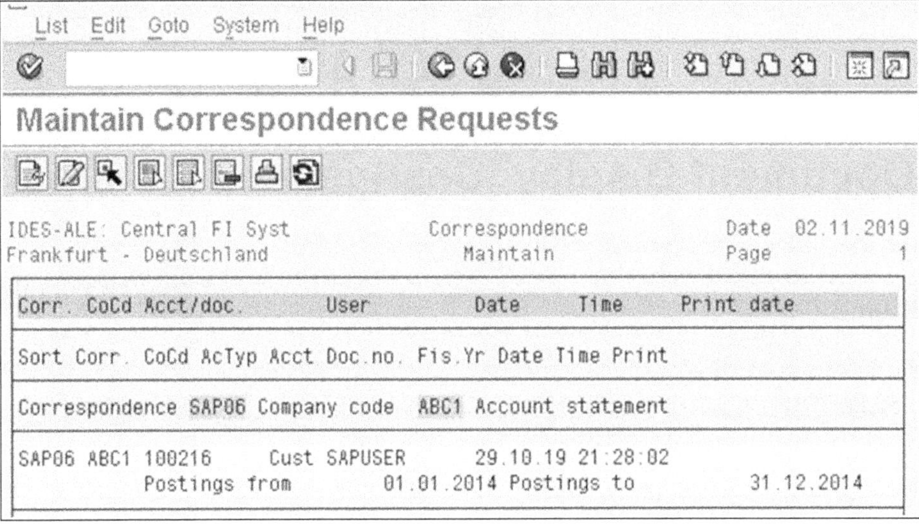

Using **TCode F.64,** we can activate the 'requests' already created to print the documents. We can also delete a document print request that we don't want.

Using TCode F.64, we can display, print, or delete document requests.

∞

We've learned Document Posting TCodes. In the next chapter, we will learn Document Display, Change, and Reversal.

∞∞

CHAPTER 6

Document Display, Change, and Reversal

We may want to visually check a posted system document and later change or reverse that document.

Let us learn how to display, change, what changes the system allows, and the methods of reversing.

Chapter Contents

∞

1. Document Display

i) Document Display TCode

FB03 - Document Display

We can display GL, AR, or AP documents using the TCode FB03.

If we have the document number, we can enter and display the document. We can also find any required document through the button option 'Document List.'

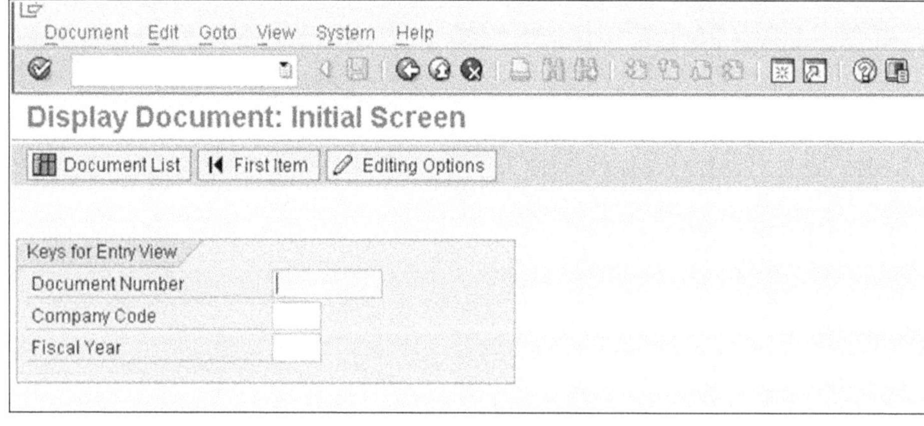

ii) Displaying Related Documents

Whenever the system interfaces transactions to the GL from other modules, it creates a document in the GL. Thus, for such interfaced GL documents, there is a corresponding **related document** in the other module.

We can display the related documents using the relationship browser.

Display the GL document using the TCode **FB03**, then go to:

> **Main Menu: Environment >> Document Environment >> Relationship Browser**

Related document example:

Consider the SD modules sales transactions interfaced to GL.

For a sales invoice in the GL sales account, there is a billing document in the SD module. We can view both documents using the relationship browser.

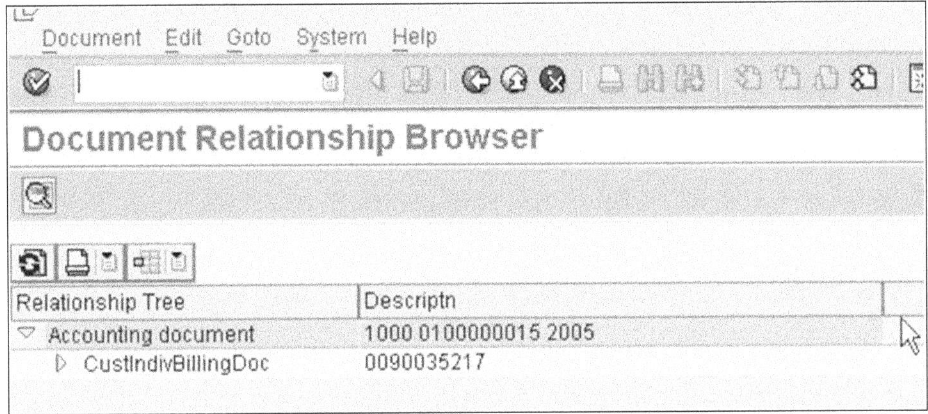

∞

2. Changing Documents

The system allows only limited options to change a document. Limiting the document change options is needed because permitting uncontrolled changes can be disastrous from the internal control perspective.

Let's learn now what changes are allowed in a document change transaction and how we can carry out those changes.

i) Changing the Document Header

FB02 - Document Change

Main Menu: Go To >> Document Header

Using this TCode, we can change **GL, AR, & AP documents**.

In a document header, we can change:

- ✓ The header text and
- ✓ The reference field content

The reference field is for entering the external reference during data entry. For example, for a vendor invoice, the vendor invoice number is the external reference.

Consider a scenario: we entered an incorrect invoice number in the reference field at the time of data entry. Now we can change it using TCode FB02.

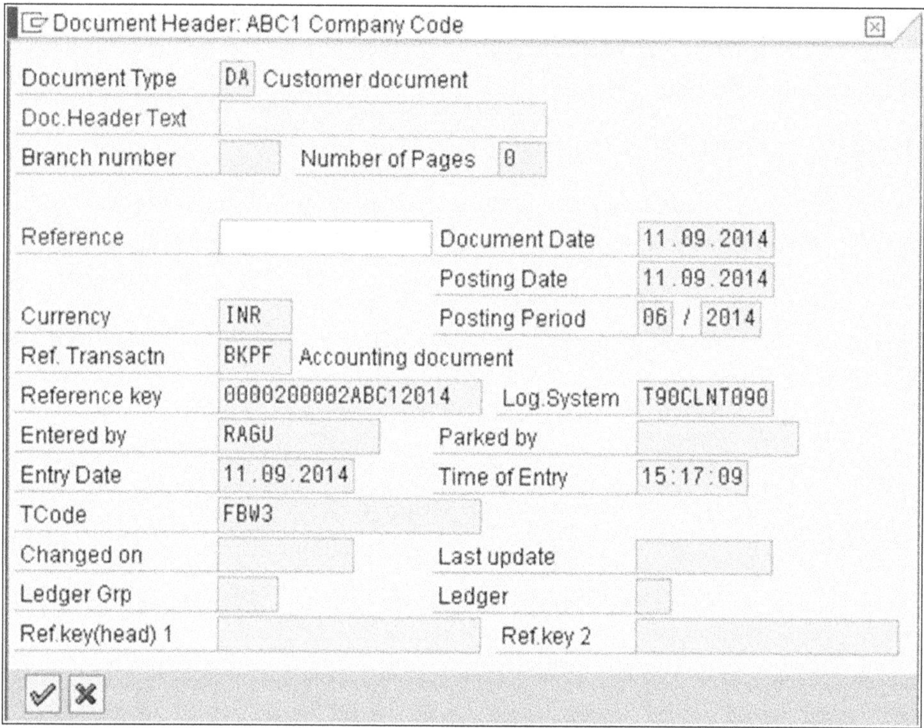

ii) Changing the Document Line Item Information

We cannot change the **account number** and the **amount**.

We can change:

- ✓ The value date,
- ✓ The assignment field, and
- ✓ The text field content.

Choose a line item and double click to open it to make any of the above changes.

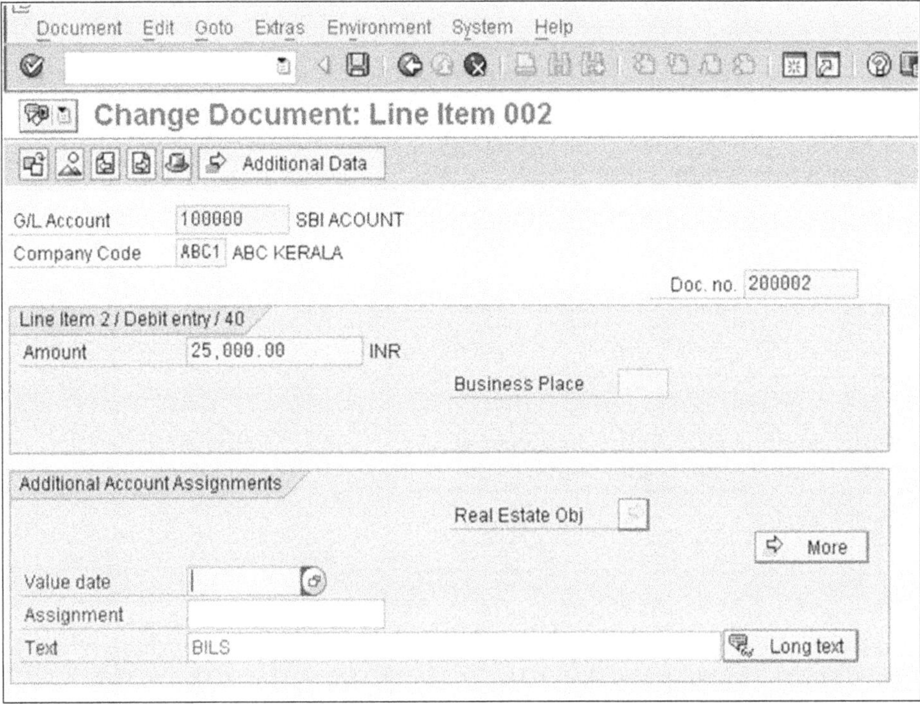

Mass Changes

GL: FBL3N - Display/Change Line Items

AR: FBL5N - Display/Change Line Items

AP: FBL1N - Display/Change Line Items

Main Menu: Environment >> Mass Change >> New Values

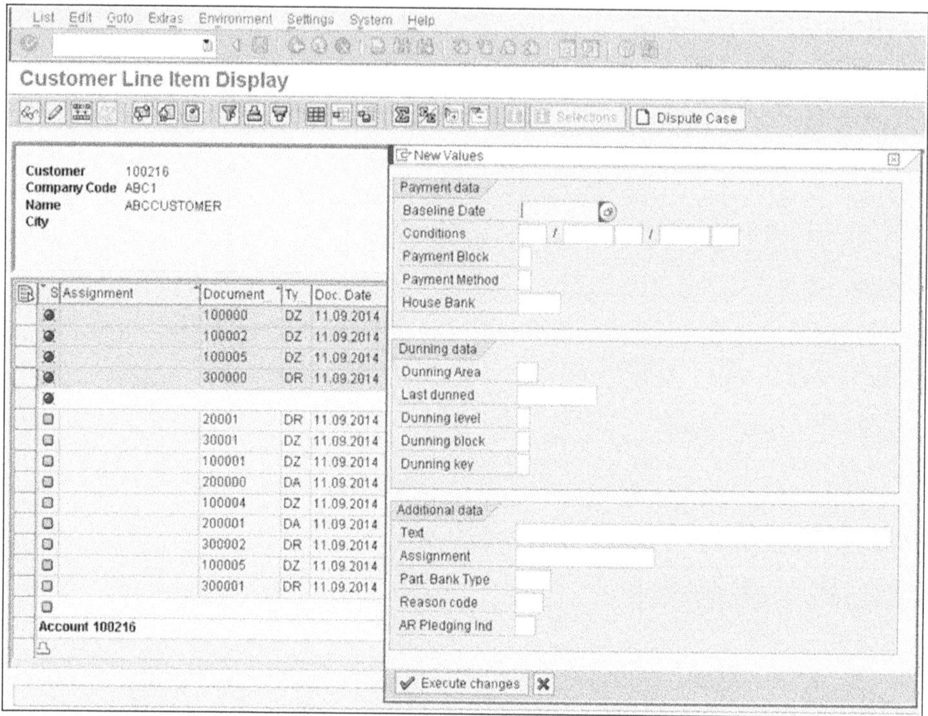

Using these TCodes, go to the required line items. Choose the line items by clicking in the left-most boxes holding the shift key.

Then go to Main Menu: Environment >> Mass Change >> New Values

Enter the new values.

For example, we can insert a new date for the 'Baseline Date' field of the selected line items all at once.

A baseline date is a date that the system refers to for determining the invoice due dates as per the payment terms.

∞

3. Document Reversal

i) Negative Posting

Negative posting is a particular method of document reversal. In a negative posting of a document reversal, the system posts a negative amount in the same debit or the credit side of the original entry.

Example:

Consider the original entry of the document as:

ABC Ltd, Customer A/c	Dr 1000
Sales A/c	Cr 1000

Entry by negative posting reversal is:

Customer ABC	Dr -1000 *(that is, minus amount, debit side)*
Sales	Cr -1000 *(that is, minus amount, credit side)*

The negative posting has a clear advantage. The sum of debit or the credit side remains the same after you reversed a document as if you've never posted that document in the system.

ii) Reversal - Post with Reference Function

FB50 - Enter G/L Account Document

FB70 - Customer Invoice

FB60 - Vendor Invoice

Main Menu: Go To >> Post with Reference

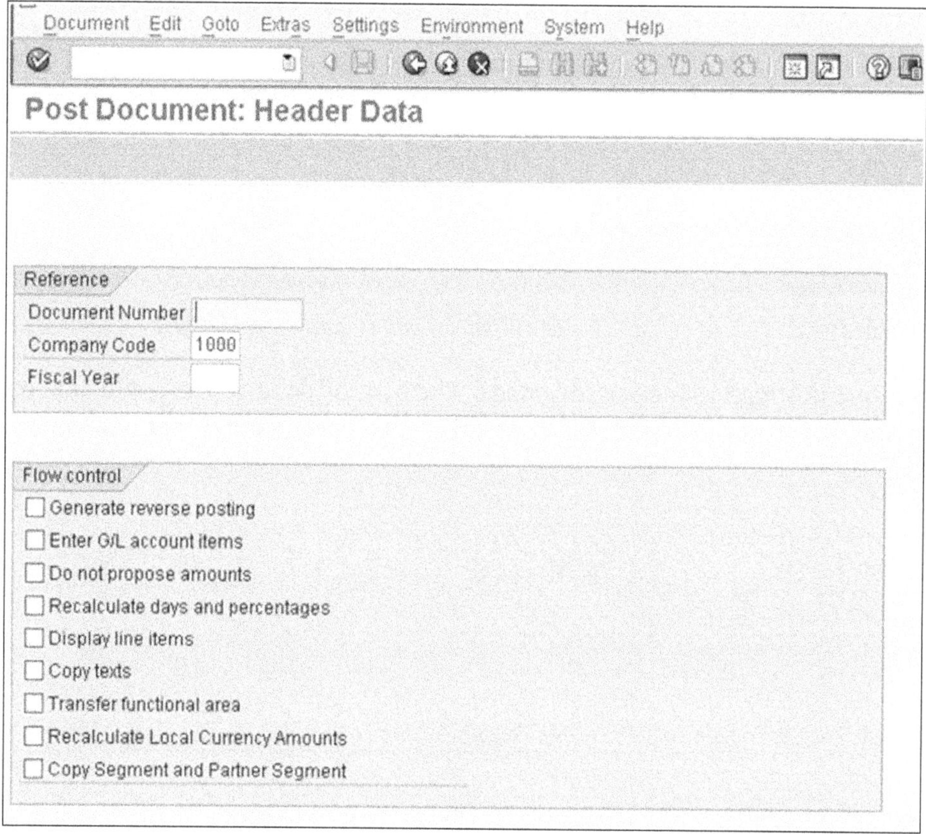

Input the document number to be reversed in the reference: document number field.

Under **Flow control,** Select the check-box 'Generate Reverse Posting' and save it. The system generates the reverse posting.

Using this reversal method, we can't do the negative posting.

We will now discuss other document reversal functions where we can reverse with negative posting.

iii) Individual Document Reversal

FB08 - Individual Reversal

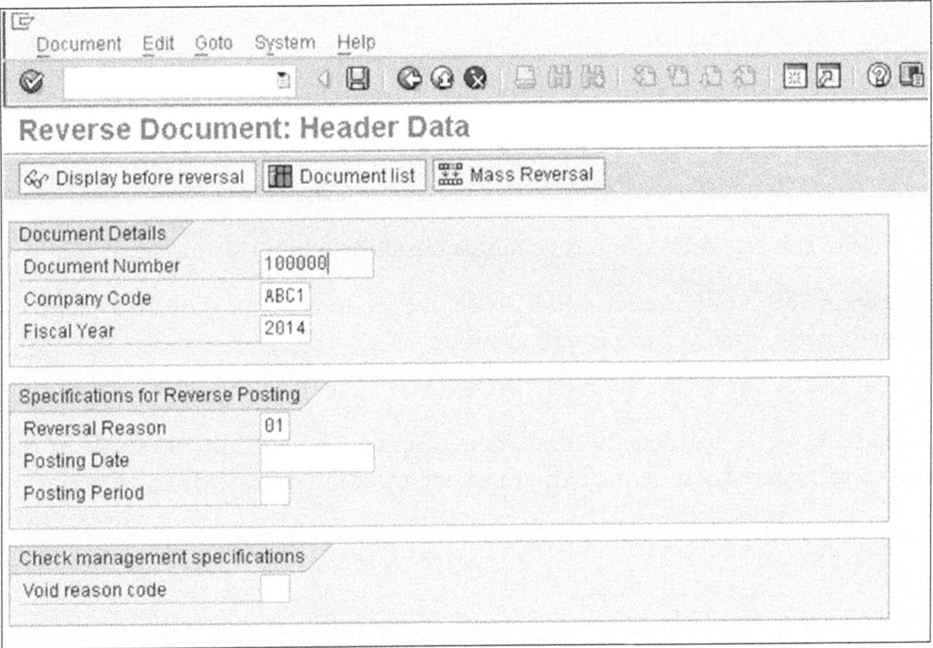

We can reverse **GL, AR, AP Documents** using the TCode FB08 by assigning a 'reversal reason code.'

Reversal Reason Code

Reverse reason code configuration determines:

1) The posting date of the reversal document, and
2) If the reversal document is a negative posting or regular posting

The system comes with a set of predefined reversal reason codes:

Reason	Text	Posting
01	Reversal in current period	Normal posting
03	Reversal in current period	Negative posting
04	Reversal in closed-period	Negative posting,

We have the option to 'Display before a reversal,' we can review the reversal, and if found to be correct, post the reversal document.

iv) Mass Reversal

F.80 - Mass Reversal

Use TCode F.80 for Mass Reversal.

We can 'test run' the mass reversal. If the test results are satisfactory, we can run again in an update mode to complete the mass reversal.

v) Check reversal and Void Reason Code

We use a 'void reason code' when reversing a check payment document.

We can create the 'void reason codes' with the system support team's help, such as printed incorrectly, stolen, and sample printout.

∞

In this chapter, we've learned the document display, change, and reversal. In the next chapter, we will learn document clearing to keep our system records clean and tidy.

∞∞

CHAPTER 7

Document Clearing

We know clearing in the system context is the process of matching off related debit and credit items.

Entries for sales and purchase are open items initially. When we receive payment against the sales, we enter the amount and match it with the sales entry, and both the sales and the payment entries get squared off or closed in the system.

Similarly, we close a purchase entry in the system with the corresponding payment entry.

Let us learn the clearing process, including automatic clearing in GR/IR account.

Chapter Contents

∞

1. GL Accounts Clearing

We have intermediary accounts in the GL. We post entries, which are squared off later with further postings.

For example, the system credits salaries as per payroll to the 'payroll clearing account.' Later, when we pay the salaries, we debit the payroll clearing account.

Other examples of GL intermediary accounts are:

- ✓ Outstanding liabilities accounts such as rent payable account
- ✓ Suspense accounts

We can square off the entries posted to such accounts using the clearing process.

i) Posting with Clearing

F-04 - Post with Clearing

Using TCode F-04, we can pay towards current liabilities like rent or receive payments towards other receivables.

During the payment entry posting of an outstanding liability, click the button 'Choose open items' to square off the payment against the liability.

ii) Manual Account Clearing

F-03 - Clear GL Account

We can use TCode F-03 to clear items that were not cleared during the transaction posting.

∞

2. Customers & Vendors Account Manual Clearing

We know that invoices are cleared with payment entries posting in the customers' and vendors' accounts. However, there are scenarios where we need to manually clear items in customers' and vendors' accounts.

For example, a customer invoice and a credit note against that invoice need clearing.

We can use the manual clearing TCodes to clear them.

The TCodes

F-32 - Clear Customer A/c

F-44 - Clear Vendor A/c

We can square off the invoice and the related credit note with the manual account clearing TCode F-32 or F-44.

The customers' and vendors' account manual clearing is very similar to the GL account manual clearing.

∞

3. Clearing: When the Customer Is Also a Vendor

The customer is also a vendor is a unique scenario, where the customer is also supplying goods or services as a vendor.

We have receivable in the customer account and payable invoices in the vendor account.

We can link such a customer and the vendor accounts and square off the customer invoice against the vendor invoice in the system.

Link the Customer and the Vendor Accounts

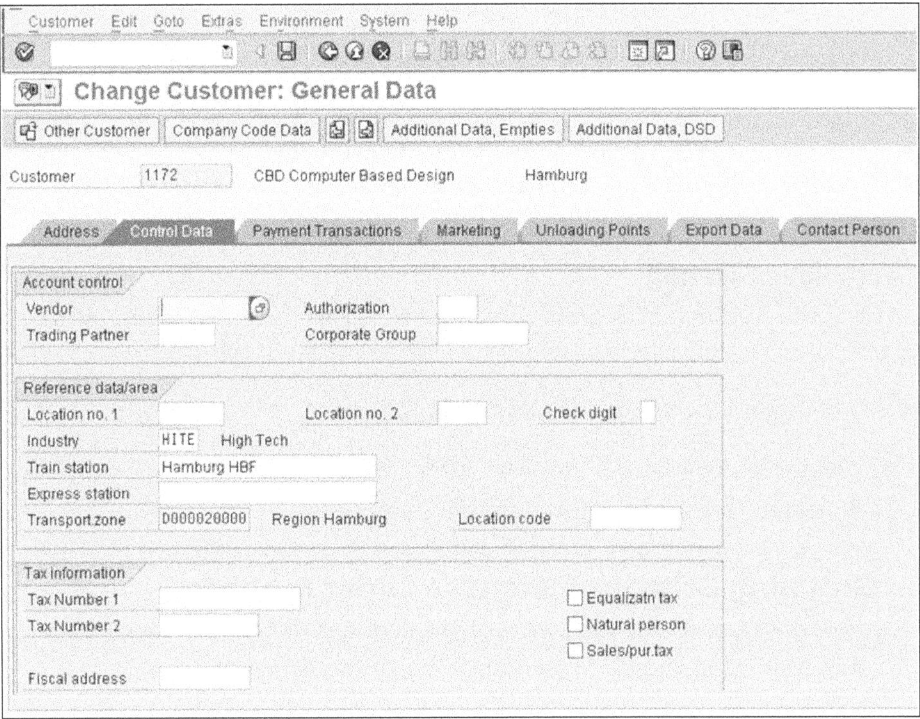

Step 1: Enter the vendor account number in the 'vendor field' in the General Data, Control Section

Step 2: Choose 'Clrg with vend.' in the Company Code Data

Save the Customer master.

Repeat the process in the vendor master: enter the customer account number in the 'customer field' and choose 'Clrg with vend' and save the vendor master.

Now the system is ready to set off vendor account invoices with customer account invoices.

We can use **manual account clearing TCode F-32** to clear the outstanding balances in the customer and vendor accounts.

4. GR/IR Account Clearing

GR/IR Account is a transitory account. We post receipt of goods and the corresponding vendor invoices to the GR/IR account and clear them with the purchase order number as the matching parameter.

However, we may not clear the entries during the posting for many reasons. This leads to the accumulation of open items in the GR/IR account.

We can classify the open items into two groups:

i) Items with negligible difference amount and

ii) Items that need clarification from the Stores and the vendors.

i) Items with negligible difference amount - Automatic Clearing

F.13 - Automatic Clearing

We can use the automatic clearing function to clear the open items with a small difference.

We need to configure the automatic clearing function for:

a) The grouping criteria - Purchase Order number, and

b) Tolerance Limits for small difference amounts

a) The Grouping Criteria - Purchase Order Number

We know that the system clears the invoice amount and the goods receipt amount for a particular purchase order number when both the amounts match.

We need to configure the purchase order number as the grouping criteria. This is a technical step. Please take the system support team's help to make the necessary configuration.

b) Tolerance Limits

Tolerance limits are another tweak that can help to clear the majority of open items. Tolerance limits definition enables the system to clear entries when there is a small difference.

Run the 'F.13 Automatic Clearing' program in test mode to get the list of items that cannot cleared. A study of the entries that the system cannot clear gives you an indication of the entries with small differences.

Depending on the analysis of the small differences that stop the clearing, we can request the system support team to define 'tolerance limits.'

When defining the tolerance limits, please check if the limit definition is working according to your expectations.

Run Automatic Clearing

After completing the two steps, namely, defining the grouping criteria for the purchase order number and the tolerance limits for small differences, we can run the automatic clearing program in **test mode**. When the results of test mode running produce no error status, we can run it in an **update mode**.

ii) Items that need clarification from the Stores and the vendors

After the automatic clearing, you may still find open items in the account.

For such open items, we need to investigate the reasons; we need to collaborate with the Purchase department, Stores where the goods are received, and the vendor to sort out the issues.

Based on the outcome of the investigation, we can carry out the corrections in the system using:

1) **Credit memo**, where there is a difference in amount due to variation in quantity, and
2) **Subsequent debit or subsequent credit** when there is a difference in amount without any quantity difference.

∞

5. Reset Cleared Items

We may come across a situation where the clearing done earlier needs a correction. For example, we have squared off the invoices with an incorrect payment. Now, we want to reverse the clearing and re-do the clearing with correct invoices and payments.

We can reverse the clearing in the system using the function **'Reset Cleared Items.'**

The TCode

FBRA - Reset Cleared Items

We can use this TCode for resetting cleared items in all types of Accounts, GL, AR & AP

To reset, enter the document number, company code, and the fiscal year. We have an option to recheck the document by clicking the 'Items' button.

Proceed to 'Save' the transaction.

We have two options: one, resetting only, and second, resetting and reversing, which will 'reverse' the clearing document.

This TCode reverts the cleared items to their original open item state. After resetting, we can 'clear' the items with the correct invoices and the payment.

6. Tit-Bits in Clearing

i) Query to Display Cleared Documents

FB03 - Document Display

Main Menu: Environment >> Payment Usage

Consider a clearing document squaring off multiple entries in the system.

We can query the system to see all the entries that were closed with a specific clearing document.

To display the clearing document, use TCode FB03, go to Main Menu: Environment >> Payment Usage.

The system gives the list of line items closed under the clearing document.

ii) System Terminology

Let's understand the **SAP System terminology** for the clearing functions with an illustration:

Consider the transaction: sales & customer payment towards the sales entries.

Clearing Document: 'Payment entry' is the clearing document.

Clearing Document Number: The 'payment entry document number' is the clearing document number.

Clearing Date: The 'payment entry date' is the clearing date.

In our example, the system updates the clearing document number and the clearing date in the sales entry.

∞

We've completed the Document Clearing chapter. In the next chapter, we will learn how to generate account balances reports, account statements, Balance Sheet, and Profit and Loss Account.

∞∞

CHAPTER 8

Account Balances, Account Statements, and more

The system comes with robust features for generating accounting reports. There are many TCodes for generating the reports; we will learn the most useful ones in this chapter.

Chapter Contents

1. Creating & Using Worklist
2. GL Account Balances
3. GL Account Statements
4. AR & AP Account Balances
5. AR & AP Account Statements
6. Standard Evaluations for AR & AP Account Analysis
7. Periodic Account Statements To Customers & Vendors, and
8. Balance Sheet & Profit & Loss A/c
9. Dynamic Selections - Useful Standard Report Filter Options
10. Background Processing

1. Creating & Using Worklist

Worklists help generate system reports for a set of customers, vendors, or GL accounts. In this first topic on system reports, let us learn how to create and use worklists.

The 'worklist' is the list of selected customer accounts, vendor accounts, or GL Accounts. A worklist is a custom list we create.

Worklists are helpful when we have a large customer or vendor portfolio, and we want to divide and delegate the customer or vendor management task to different accounting clerks.

In this scenario, each staff member can create a worklist of customers or vendors they are responsible. Worklists make life easy for them to work with the system as they can now refer to the worklist instead of individual customers or vendors for querying the system for open items.

We can create as many worklists as needed for GL Accounts, customers, and vendors.

i) Creating Worklists

S_ALR_87005102 - Maintain Worklist for Processing Open Items

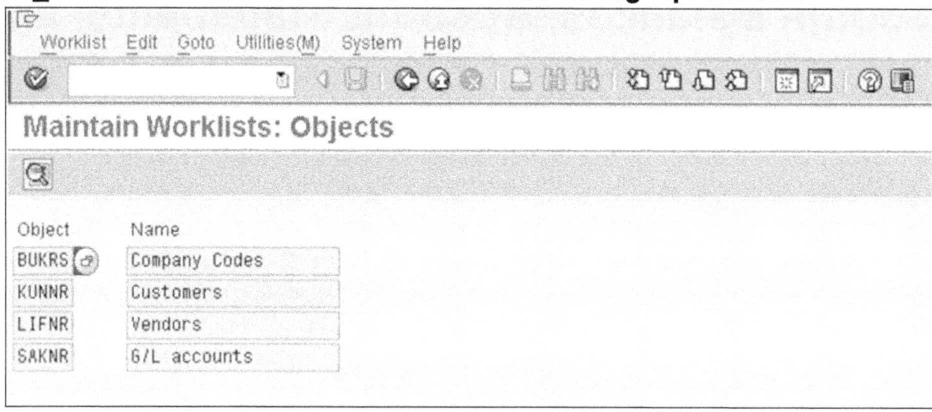

Using this TCode, you can create a worklist for customers, vendors, and GL accounts.

ii) Setting up the System to Use Worklists

FB00 - Editing Options

Go to: Line Items Tab

You need to enable the system to use the worklist function. The worklist function can be enabled or disabled for the individual user.

To enable the worklists, type the TCode: FB00 in the Command-Line and go to the Line Items Tab.

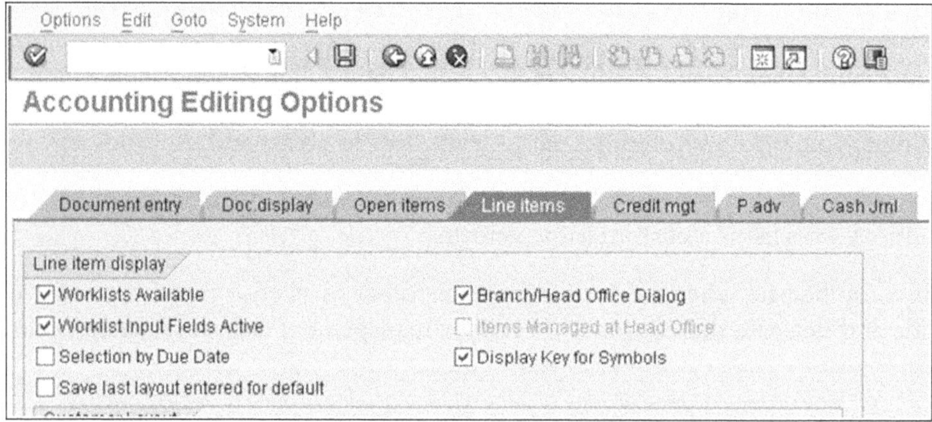

1. Select **Worklists Available** checkbox and **'save'** then,
(next option would be available for selection after you 'save' your choice now)
2. Select **Worklist Input Fields Active** checkbox and again **'save.'**

After enabling this, we can **define worklists and use them** in queries, where the system has the worklist option.

Example:

TCode: FBL5N - Display/Change Line Items

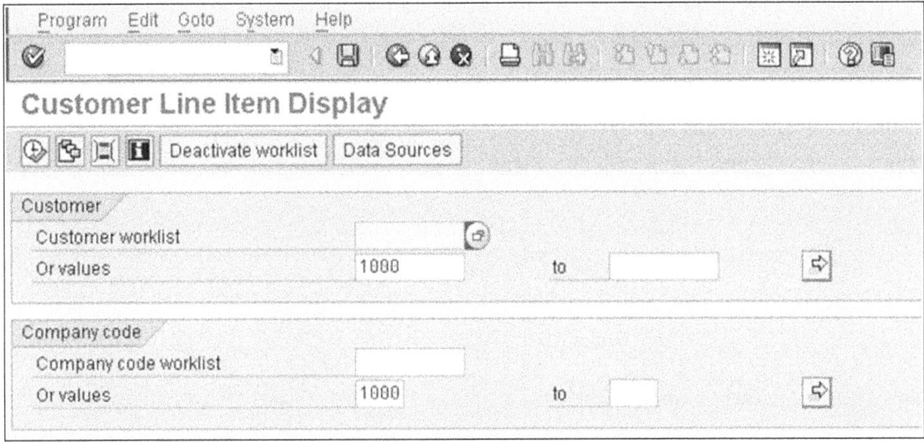

iii) System Queries With Worklist Option

- ✓ GL: FBL3N - Display /Change Line Items
- ✓ AR: FBL5N - Display /Change Line Items
- ✓ AP: FBL1N - Display /Change Line Items
- ✓ AR: FD11 - Analysis

∞

2. G/L Account Balances

i) Period-wise Account Balances

FS10N - Display GL Account Balances

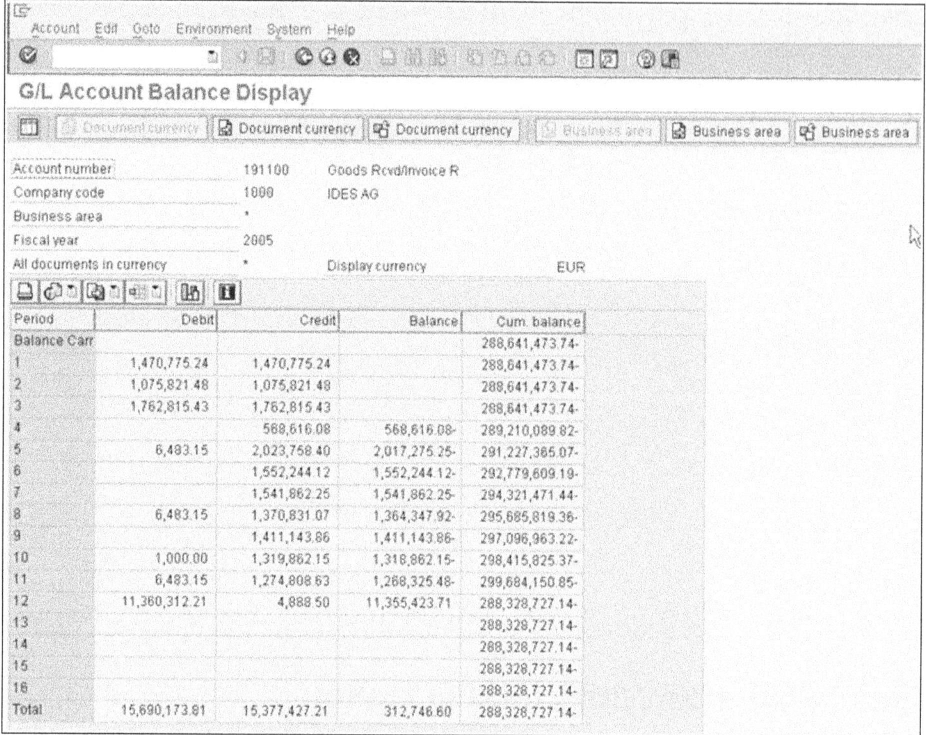

Account number 191100 Goods Rcvd/Invoice R
Company code 1000 IDES AG
Business area *
Fiscal year 2005
All documents in currency * Display currency EUR

Period	Debit	Credit	Balance	Cum. balance
Balance Carr				288,641,473.74-
1	1,470,775.24	1,470,775.24		288,641,473.74-
2	1,075,821.48	1,075,821.48		288,641,473.74-
3	1,762,815.43	1,762,815.43		288,641,473.74-
4		568,616.08	568,616.08-	289,210,089.82-
5	6,483.15	2,023,758.40	2,017,275.25-	291,227,365.07-
6		1,552,244.12	1,552,244.12-	292,779,609.19-
7		1,541,862.25	1,541,862.25-	294,321,471.44-
8	6,483.15	1,370,831.07	1,364,347.92-	295,685,819.36-
9		1,411,143.86	1,411,143.86-	297,096,963.22-
10	1,000.00	1,319,862.15	1,318,862.15-	298,415,825.37-
11	6,483.15	1,274,808.63	1,268,325.48-	299,684,150.85-
12	11,360,312.21	4,888.50	11,355,423.71	288,328,727.14-
13				288,328,727.14-
14				288,328,727.14-
15				288,328,727.14-
16				288,328,727.14-
Total	15,690,173.81	15,377,427.21	312,746.60	288,328,727.14-

FS10N report gives you period-wise

1) Total Debit,
2) Total Credit,
3) Net-balance, and
4) Cumulative Balance values.

FS10N is a drill-down report. From this account balances report, you can go to the line item reports or display a document.

ii) Trial Balance Report

S_ALR_87012277 - G/L Account Balances

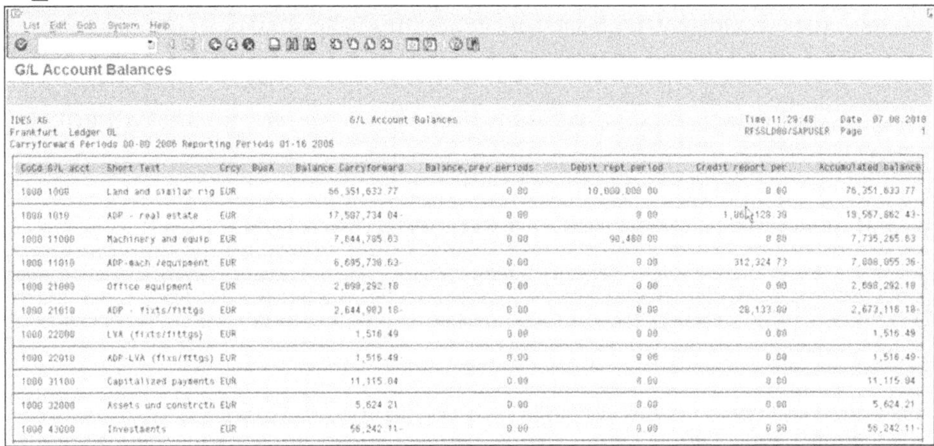

G/L Account Balances

IDES AG — G/L Account Balances — Time 11:29:48 Date 07.08.2018
Frankfurt Ledger 0L — RFSSLD00/SAPUSER Page 1
Carryforward Periods 00-00 2006 Reporting Periods 01-16 2006

CoCd	G/L acct	Short Text	Crcy	BusA	Balance Carryforward	Balance,prev.periods	Debit rept.period	Credit report per.	Accumulated balance
1000	1000	Land and similar rig	EUR		66,351,633.77	0.00	10,000,000.00	0.00	76,351,633.77
1000	1010	ADP - real estate	EUR		17,587,734.04-	0.00	0.00	1,86[illegible]128.39	19,587,862.43-
1000	11000	Machinery and equip	EUR		7,644,785.63	0.00	90,480.00	0.00	7,735,265.63
1000	11010	ADP-mach./equipment	EUR		6,695,730.63-	0.00	0.00	312,324.73	7,008,055.36-
1000	21000	Office equipment	EUR		2,898,292.18	0.00	0.00	0.00	2,898,292.18
1000	21010	ADP - fixts/fittgs	EUR		2,644,983.18-	0.00	0.00	28,133.00	2,673,116.18-
1000	22000	LVA (fixts/fittgs)	EUR		1,516.49	0.00	0.00	0.00	1,516.49
1000	22010	ADP-LVA (fixs/fttgs)	EUR		1,516.49-	0.00	0.00	0.00	1,516.49-
1000	31100	Capitalized payments	EUR		11,115.04	0.00	0.00	0.00	11,115.04
1000	32000	Assets und constrctn	EUR		5,624.21	0.00	0.00	0.00	5,624.21
1000	43000	Investments	EUR		56,242.11-	0.00	0.00	0.00	56,242.11-

We often require a Trial Balance report from the system. We can generate the Trial Balance report for one or more periods or a fiscal year.

A Trial Balance is the complete list of GL Accounts with *Beginning Balance, Debits during the Period, Credits During The Period, and Ending Balance.*

Next, we will learn how to extract **GL Account Statements.**

∞

3. GL Account Statements

i) Statement of Accounts

FBL3N - Display /Change Line Items

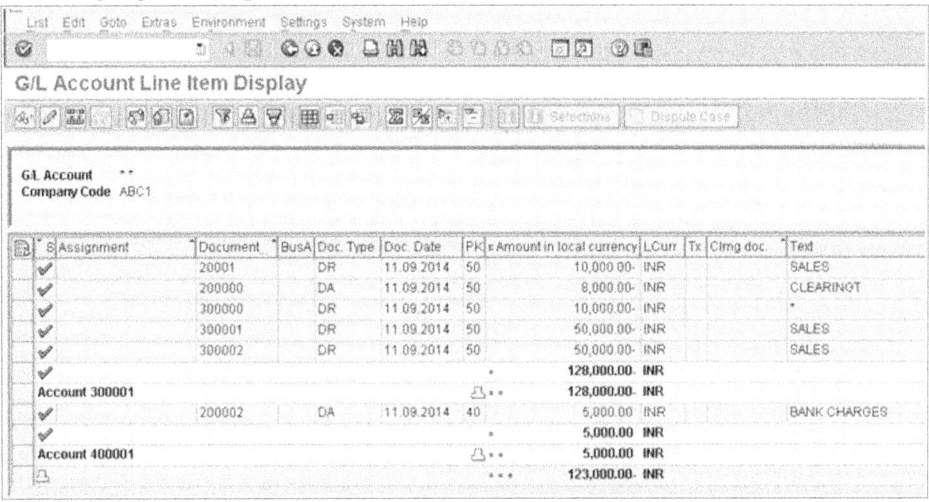

G/L Account Line Item Display

G/L Account **
Company Code ABC1

S	Assignment	Document	BusA	Doc. Type	Doc. Date	PK	Amount in local currency	LCurr	Tx	Clrng doc.	Text
✔		20001		DR	11.09.2014	50	10,000.00-	INR			SALES
✔		200000		DA	11.09.2014	50	8,000.00-	INR			CLEARINGT
✔		300000		DR	11.09.2014	50	10,000.00-	INR			*
✔		300001		DR	11.09.2014	50	50,000.00-	INR			SALES
✔		300002		DR	11.09.2014	50	50,000.00-	INR			SALES
✔						•	**128,000.00-**	**INR**			
Account 300001						••	**128,000.00-**	**INR**			
✔		200002		DA	11.09.2014	40	5,000.00	INR			BANK CHARGES
✔						•	**5,000.00**	**INR**			
Account 400001						••	**5,000.00**	**INR**			
						•••	**123,000.00-**	**INR**			

Using the TCode FBL3N, we can generate the GL account line items report. We can generate the FBL3N report for one or more GL accounts.

We can use the worklist function for generating the FBL3N report. The system generates a report with line items and a summary sheet.

FBL3N is a drill-down report; we can drill down to go to **Document Display /Change.**

ii) An All-in-one Statement of Accounts Report

S_ALR_87012332 - Account Statements

This is an excellent report to extract Account Statements for your GL accounts, customers' accounts, or vendors' accounts.

It has powerful options for filtering the output. Interestingly, we can even filter by cost center and by the plant.

The report options are:

1) Standard Documents,
2) Parked Documents,
3) Noted Items, and
4) Recurring Entry original documents.

Item selection 1,2,3: All Items, Cleared Items, and Open Items

I encourage you to explore the remaining options to appreciate the power of this report program to give you the output you want.

4. AR & AP Account Balances

i) Query For Account Balances

FD10N - Display Customers A/c Balances

FK10N - Display Vendors A/c Balances

We can generate account balances for a list of customers' or vendors' accounts.

The system generates reports with two tabs:

1) Normal Balances, and
2) Special GL Balances.

Let's refresh now on what are '*normal*' transactions and what are '*special*' transactions.

Customer account normal transactions are sales and payment receipt against the sales, and vendor accounts normal transactions are purchases and payments against the purchases.

So, what are special transactions?

Any customer or vendor accounts transactions that are not normal transactions are special transactions.

For example, advance payments, security deposits are special transactions.

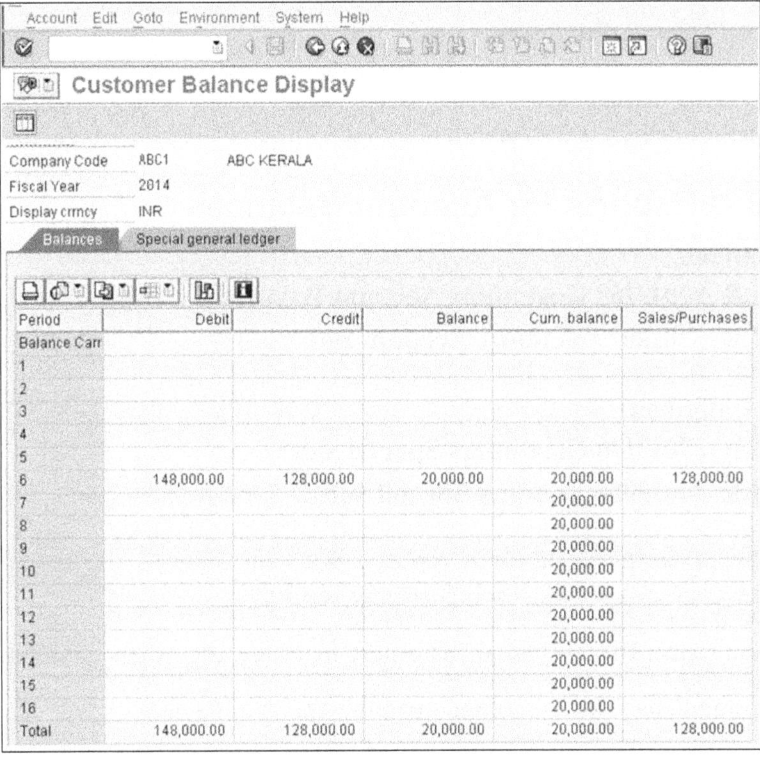

Account Edit Goto Environment System Help

Customer Balance Display

Company Code ABC1 ABC KERALA
Fiscal Year 2014
Display crrncy INR

Balances | Special general ledger

Period	Debit	Credit	Balance	Cum. balance	Sales/Purchases
Balance Carr					
1					
2					
3					
4					
5					
6	148,000.00	128,000.00	20,000.00	20,000.00	128,000.00
7				20,000.00	
8				20,000.00	
9				20,000.00	
10				20,000.00	
11				20,000.00	
12				20,000.00	
13				20,000.00	
14				20,000.00	
15				20,000.00	
16				20,000.00	
Total	148,000.00	128,000.00	20,000.00	20,000.00	128,000.00

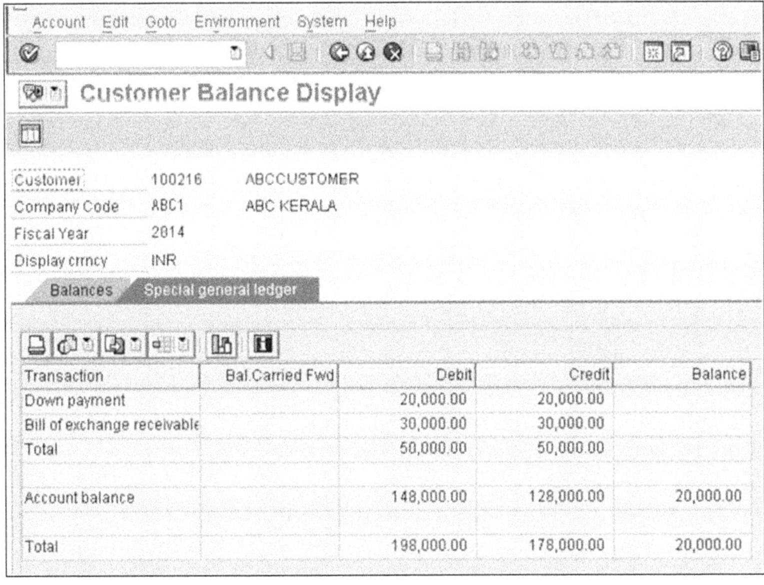

Account Edit Goto Environment System Help

Customer Balance Display

Customer 100216 ABCCUSTOMER
Company Code ABC1 ABC KERALA
Fiscal Year 2014
Display crrncy INR

Balances | Special general ledger

Transaction	Bal.Carried Fwd	Debit	Credit	Balance
Down payment		20,000.00	20,000.00	
Bill of exchange receivable		30,000.00	30,000.00	
Total		50,000.00	50,000.00	
Account balance		148,000.00	128,000.00	20,000.00
Total		198,000.00	178,000.00	20,000.00

For both normal balances and special GL balances tab, the system generates period-wise,

1) Total Debit,
2) Total Credit,
3) Cumulative Balance, and
4) Total Sales or Purchases

FD10N & FK10N reports are drill-down reports. We can drill down to the line item report and further display a document.

ii) Standard Reports for Account Balances

Normal Balances

S_ALR_87012169 Customers Account Balance

S_ALR_87012079 Vendors Account Balances

Special GL Balances

S_ALR_87012170 Customers Special Sales

S_ALR_87012080 Vendors Special Sales

These reports are a special kind of reports. We can generate the report for all the customers; then, we can browse each customer report.

How to get the report for individual customers from the customers' summary report?

Go to navigation: Select the 'customer' attribute and double click

Now we can browse through the reports of individual customers one by one.

We can also drill down **Debit, Credit & Balance columns.**

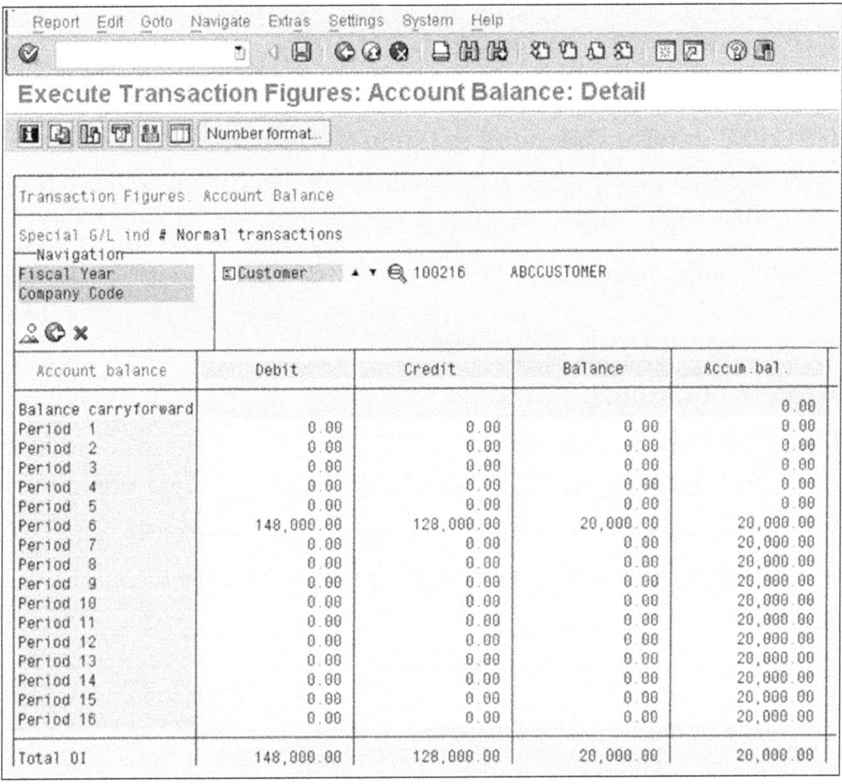

Account balance	Debit	Credit	Balance	Accum.bal.
Balance carryforward				0.00
Period 1	0.00	0.00	0.00	0.00
Period 2	0.00	0.00	0.00	0.00
Period 3	0.00	0.00	0.00	0.00
Period 4	0.00	0.00	0.00	0.00
Period 5	0.00	0.00	0.00	0.00
Period 6	148,000.00	128,000.00	20,000.00	20,000.00
Period 7	0.00	0.00	0.00	20,000.00
Period 8	0.00	0.00	0.00	20,000.00
Period 9	0.00	0.00	0.00	20,000.00
Period 10	0.00	0.00	0.00	20,000.00
Period 11	0.00	0.00	0.00	20,000.00
Period 12	0.00	0.00	0.00	20,000.00
Period 13	0.00	0.00	0.00	20,000.00
Period 14	0.00	0.00	0.00	20,000.00
Period 15	0.00	0.00	0.00	20,000.00
Period 16	0.00	0.00	0.00	20,000.00
Total OI	148,000.00	128,000.00	20,000.00	20,000.00

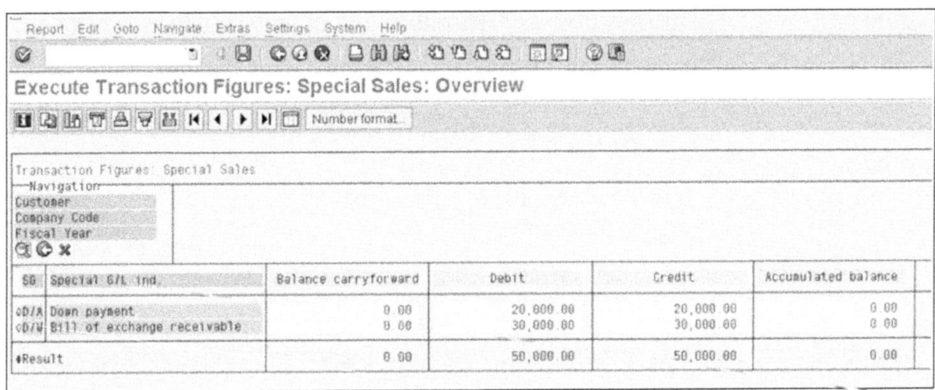

SG	Special G/L ind.	Balance carryforward	Debit	Credit	Accumulated balance
◊D/A	Down payment	0.00	20,000.00	20,000.00	0.00
◊D/W	Bill of exchange receivable	0.00	30,000.00	30,000.00	0.00
♦Result		0.00	50,000.00	50,000.00	0.00

iii) Account Balances in Local Currency

S_ALR_87012172 Customer Balances in Local Currency

S_ALR_87012082 Vendor Balances in Local Currency

Balances in local currency report is a printable report with a customer-wise beginning balance, total debits, total credits, and cumulative balance.

We can generate the report for normal balances, or Spl GL Balances, or both.

iv) Sales & Purchases Reports

S_ALR_87012186 Customer Sales

S_ALR_87012093 Vendor Business

We can generate a report using this standard report option to get the customers' sales balances or the vendors' purchase balances.

As per the standard configuration, the system captures the sales or purchase data based on document types.

For example, the sales data is captured based on:

Document Types	Description
RV	Billing doc. transfer - SD Sales
DR	Customer invoice - FI Sales
DG	Customer credit memo

Both SD module sales and sales posted in FI, less credit memo issued, are reported as sales balance.

v). Period-wise Drilldown Report

S_ALR_87012171 Sales - Customers A/cs

S_ALR_87012081 Purchases - Vendors A/cs

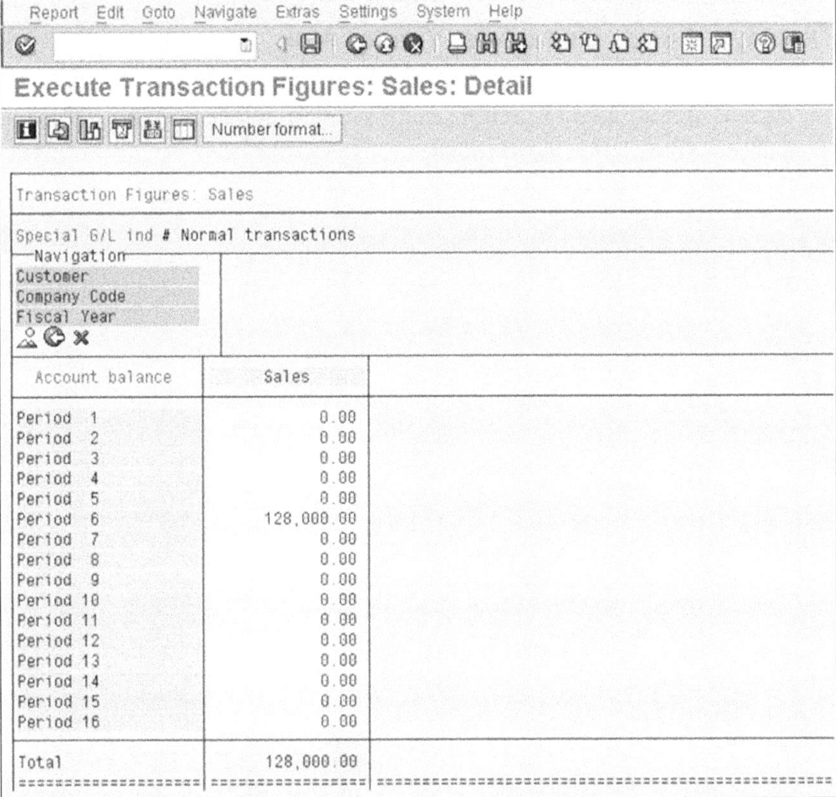

Account balance	Sales
Period 1	0.00
Period 2	0.00
Period 3	0.00
Period 4	0.00
Period 5	0.00
Period 6	128,000.00
Period 7	0.00
Period 8	0.00
Period 9	0.00
Period 10	0.00
Period 11	0.00
Period 12	0.00
Period 13	0.00
Period 14	0.00
Period 15	0.00
Period 16	0.00
Total	128,000.00

We can navigate through individual customer's or vendor's reports.

How to navigate?

Go to navigation: Select the Customer attribute or the vendor attribute and double click to go to individual customer's or vendor's report.

The customers' sales & the vendors' purchase reports are drill-down reports. We can drill down the sales or the purchases balances reports to view the details.

∞

5. AR & AP Account Statements

i) Query For Account Statements

FBL5N - Display /Change Line Items -Customer A/cs

FBL1N - Display /Change Line Items -Vendor A/cs

We can use the worklist function for the TCodes FBL5N & FBL1N. We can choose open items, cleared items, and all items. Also, we can select normal items, special GL transactions, parked items, and noted items.

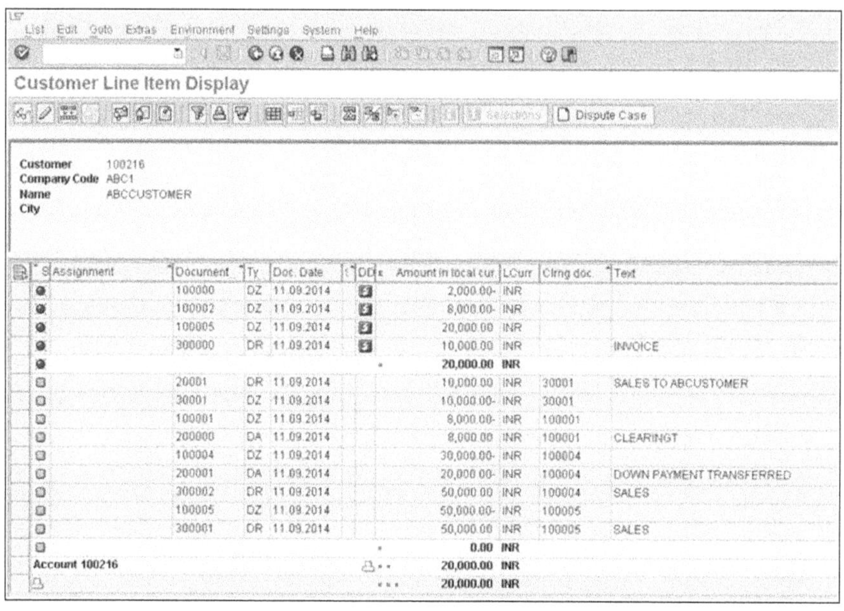

ii) Classic Line Items Display

S_ALR_87012197 List of Customer Line Items

S_ALR_87012103 List of Vendor Line Items

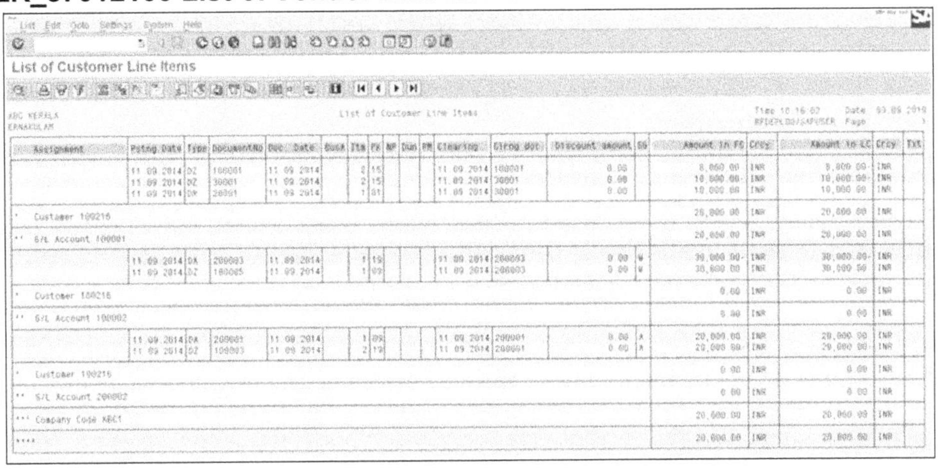

List of Customer Line Items

ABC KERALA
ERNAKULAM

List of Customer Line Items

Time 10:16:07 Date 03.09.2019
RFIEPL00/SAPUSER Page 1

Assignment	Pstng Date	Type	DocumentNo	Doc. Date	BusA	Itm	PK	NP	Dun	PM	Clearing	Clrng doc.	Discount amount	SG	Amount in FC	Crcy	Amount in LC	Crcy	Txt
	11.09.2014	DZ	100001	11.09.2014		2	15				11.09.2014	100001	0.00		8,000.00	INR	8,000.00-	INR	
	11.09.2014	DZ	30001	11.09.2014		2	15				11.09.2014	30001	0.00		10,000.00-	INR	10,000.00-	INR	
	11.09.2014	DR	20001	11.09.2014		1	01				11.09.2014	30001	0.00		10,000.00	INR	10,000.00	INR	
* Customer 100216															20,000.00	INR	20,000.00	INR	
** G/L Account 100001															20,000.00	INR	20,000.00	INR	
	11.09.2014	DA	200003	11.09.2014		1	19				11.09.2014	200003	0.00	W	30,000.00-	INR	30,000.00-	INR	
	11.09.2014	DZ	100005	11.09.2014		1	09				11.09.2014	200003	0.00	W	30,000.00	INR	30,000.00	INR	
* Customer 100216															0.00	INR	0.00	INR	
** G/L Account 100002															0.00	INR	0.00	INR	
	11.09.2014	DA	200001	11.09.2014		1	09				11.09.2014	200001	0.00	A	20,000.00	INR	20,000.00	INR	
	11.09.2014	DZ	100003	11.09.2014		2	19				11.09.2014	200001	0.00	A	20,000.00-	INR	20,000.00-	INR	
* Customer 100215															0.00	INR	0.00	INR	
** G/L Account 200002															0.00	INR	0.00	INR	
*** Company Code ABC1															20,000.00	INR	20,000.00	INR	
****															20,000.00	INR	20,000.00	INR	

We have the options to choose open items, cleared items, and all items. Also, we can select standard, parked & noted documents.

We get the output: customer name and address, customer-wise, reconciliation a/c-wise & company code-wise totals.

∞

6. Standard Evaluations for AR & AP Account Analysis

Standard evaluations for AR & AP are a versatile reporting tool in the SAP system. It is capable of producing an analytical view of customers' and vendors' transactions.

As per SAP definition, an evaluation is a dataset we select and summarize according to predefined rules.

The system stores the 'evaluation' in a table. We can draw an analytical report from the evaluation quickly without inputting any parameters as the data is available in a database table ready to be retrieved.

Who creates the evaluation?

Creating an evaluation is a technical job. Therefore, take the system admin team's help to create the evaluation.

When can we create the evaluation?

We can create the evaluation only after completing the period-end closing.

Also, we have to create the 'standard evaluations' for all the company codes in the system; we cannot create the evaluation for a single company code. Thus, period closing should be complete for all the company codes before creating the evaluations.

Testing the Evaluation

FBL5N - Display/Change Line Items

An evaluation is a dataset produced by the system using the AR, AP records. Let me remind you that there could be a **mismatch** of data output between the results of standard evaluations and the transaction data in the system.

These mismatches are due to, in most circumstances, incorrect definitions of '**Data Volume,**' which is one of the necessary technical steps in the creation of evaluations.

So, when the standard evaluations are ready for use, we need to test them for correctness.

We have to check the correctness of the evaluation data by extracting the FBL5N - Display/Change Line Items report and agreeing on the balances with evaluation reports.

We have to take the system support team's help to make the corrections if the two reports mismatch.

ii) Customer Information System

S_ALR_87012167 Customer Information System

Let's see evaluation reports from the system:

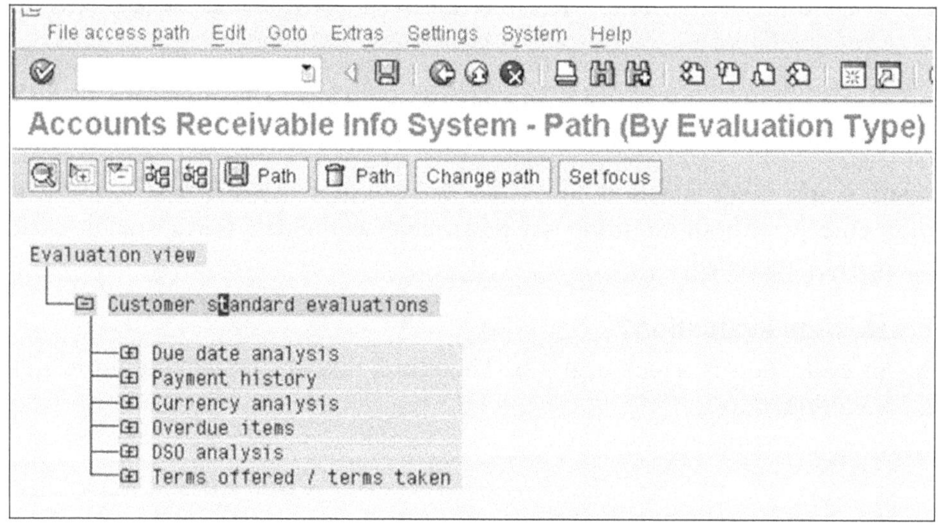

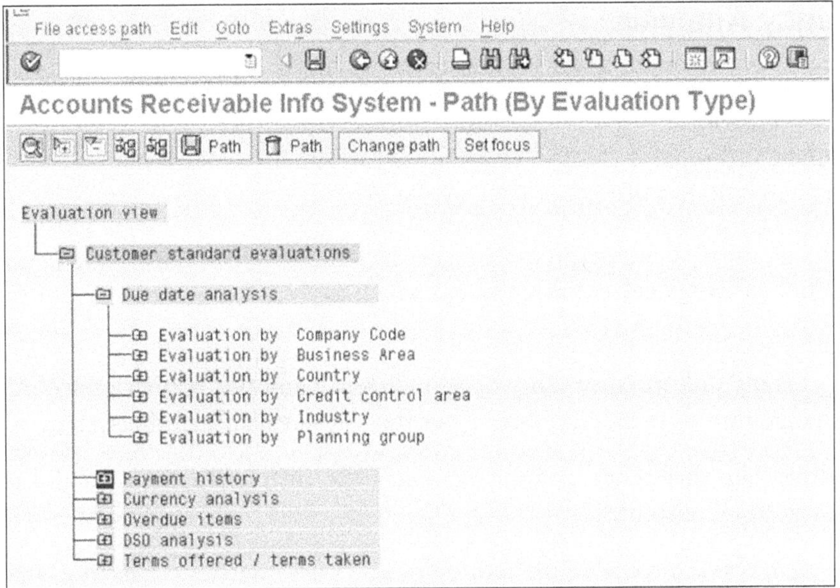

a) Due Date Analysis

The reports give three variants - **Total OIs, OIs due, OIs not due**.

Total Open Items

The report gives the company code-wise due, not due, and total open items. Choosing a company code and drill-down takes us to the customer-wise details. We can choose any one of the customers and further drill down to go the open item line report.

Open Items Due

Selecting the button 'Open OIs Due' gives an aging report, say 0-30, 31- 60, greater than 60 days.

Open Items Not Due

Similar to the 'OIs Due' report, choosing the button "OIs Not Due' gives an aging report of 'in how many days' the invoices would fall due for payment.

∞

b) Payment History

The report provides company code-wise and further drill-down reports -customer-wise,

- ✓ Days in Arrear, Medium Term,
- ✓ Days in Arrear, Short Term, and
- ✓ Days in Arrears OIs.

We can go to the line items report of a customer by further drill-down of a customer line item.

c) Currency Analysis

We get a report of each company code currency analysis:

- ✓ Total Historical,
- ✓ Total Current, and
- ✓ Exchange Rate Difference for Current

The 'total historical' column gives foreign currency amounts converted to company code currency at historical currency rates, which are exchange rates at the transaction dates.

The 'total current' column gives the foreign currency amount converted to CC currency at the exchange rate as at the key date as per the rates available in the system.

The exchange rate difference column provides the difference between the two, 'total historical' and 'total current.'

Drilldown of a company code line item gives you customer-wise currency analysis, and we can go to the line item report of any chosen customer line item.

d) Overdue Items

This report provides interest calculation for overdue items if the system is configured to charge interest on overdue items.

e) DSO Analysis

We get the 'days sales outstanding' based on current year sales. The outstanding amount is divided by average sales per day to give you the DSO days.

iii) Vendor Information System

S_ALR_87012077 Vendor Information System

- ✓ Due Date Analysis
- ✓ Currency Analysis
- ✓ Overdue Items

The report output for each report variant is the same as we discussed under Account Analysis for Customers.

∞

7. Periodic Account Statements to Customers and Vendors

We want to send account statements to the customers and vendors in a letter format every month.

We can print any of the 'predefined' correspondence types like 'SAP06 Statement of Account' or 'SAP08 Open Items List' in two steps.

Step 1: Update the customer or the vendor master record for whom we want to send the periodic account statements.

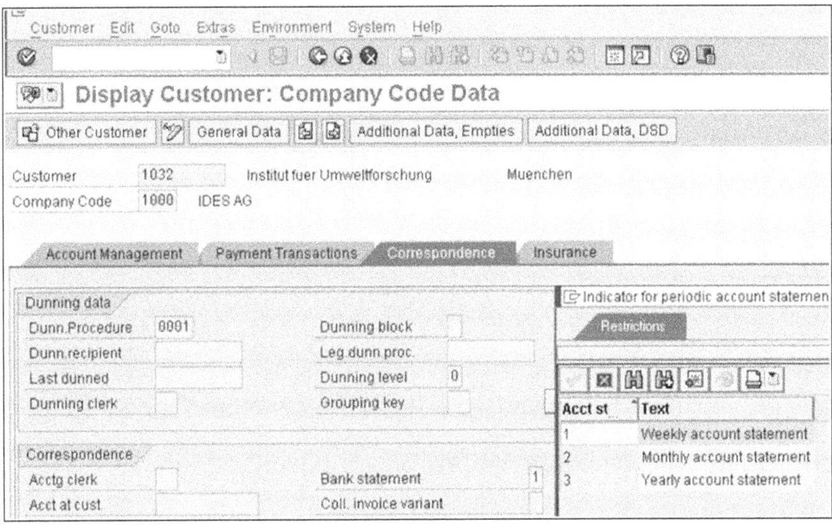

Update master record: company code data - correspondence tab: correspondence section >> bank statement

Update Field: '1' for weekly, and '2' for the monthly statement.

Step 2: Run the **TCode F.27 - Periodic Account Statements**

The system generates a print spool request, which we can print and send out to the customers and vendors. The system prints the account statements for the customers and the vendors whose bank statement field in the master data is updated, as we discussed.

∞

8. Balance Sheet & Profit & Loss Account

We can draw the company code Balance Sheet and Profit and Loss Accounts with this standard report.

S_ALR_87012284 - Financial Statement

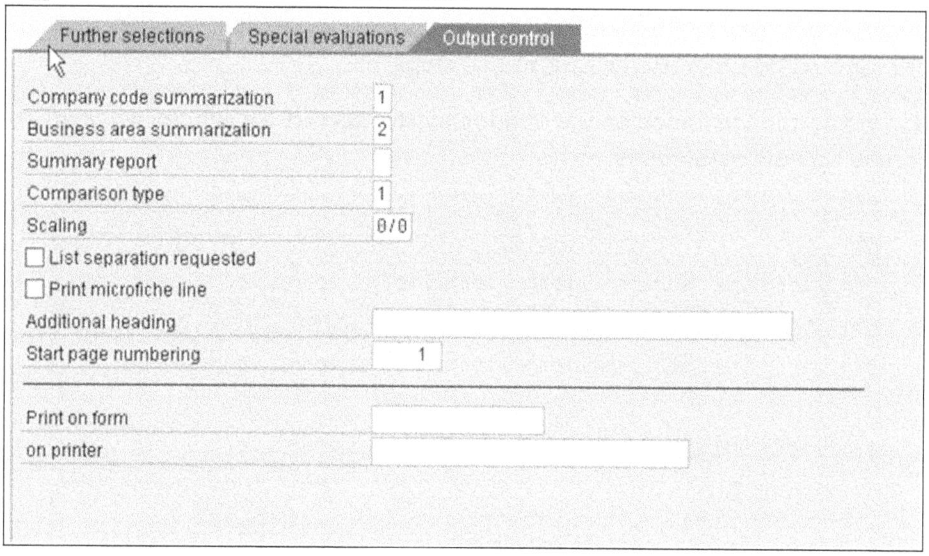

Further selections | Special evaluations | Output control

Company code summarization	1
Business area summarization	2
Summary report	
Comparison type	1
Scaling	0/0
☐ List separation requested	
☐ Print microfiche line	
Additional heading	
Start page numbering	1
Print on form	
on printer	

We can draw the Financial Statements with different summarization levels.

To get the summary report: choose the first option under 'list output.'

Go to the **output control** tab and select under summary report:

- ✓ 1 to 9: progressively detailed, 1 for highest summarization and 9 for detailed but without the GL accounts, and
- ✓ Leave the field blank for the most detailed Balance Sheet and Profit & Loss account with all the GL accounts.

∞

9. Dynamic Selections - Standard Report Filter Options

Dynamic selections are one of the most underutilized but powerful options to make specific queries in the system. 'Dynamic selections' provide a range of selection parameters to filter the report output.

Dynamic selections are additional parameter selection options in the initial screen of the standard reports.

When running a standard report in the system, we can choose the dynamic selections by following the menu path:

Main Menu: Edit >> Dynamic Selections.

Let's now learn how to use dynamic selections in real-life scenarios.

i) Report by Account Group

S_ALR_87012279 Structured Account Balances

S_ALR_87012279 Structured Account Balances report gives you the Balance Sheet and Profit and Loss Account for a company code.

Considering a scenario, we want only the accounts of the 'fixed assets account group' in this report. We can get a report with only fixed assets accounts by applying a filter in 'dynamic selections.'

Go to: Main Menu: Edit >> Dynamic Selections AND Select the 'Account Group' under GL Account Master Record.

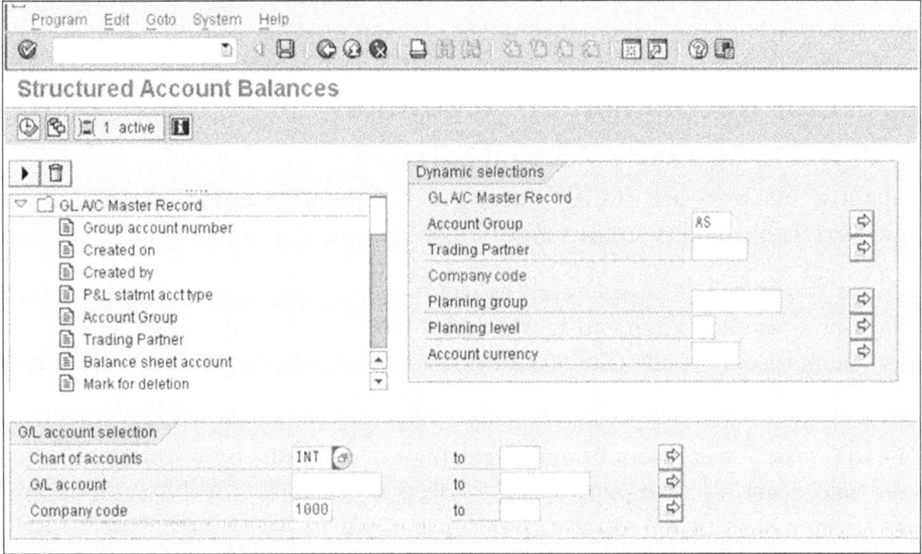

I have selected in this example scenario AS for the fixed assets account group. Now, executing the report gives the output precisely what we wanted:

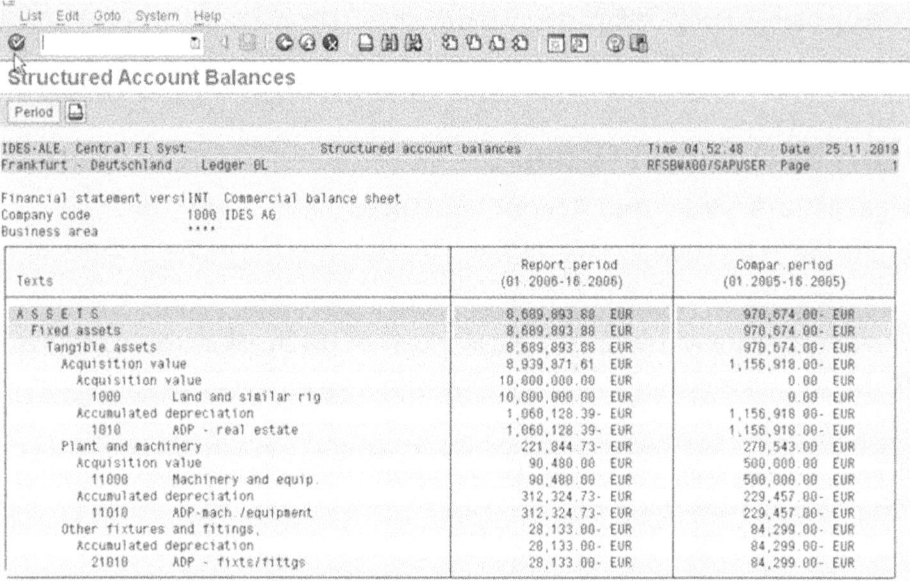

IDES-ALE Central FI Syst — Structured account balances — Time 04:52:48 Date 25.11.2019
Frankfurt - Deutschland Ledger 0L — RFSBWA00/SAPUSER Page 1

Financial statement versi INT Commercial balance sheet
Company code 1000 IDES AG
Business area ****

Texts	Report period (01.2006-16.2006)	Compar.period (01.2005-16.2005)
A S S E T S	8,689,893.88 EUR	970,674.00- EUR
Fixed assets	8,689,893.88 EUR	970,674.00- EUR
Tangible assets	8,689,893.88 EUR	970,674.00- EUR
Acquisition value	8,939,871.61 EUR	1,156,918.00- EUR
Acquisition value	10,000,000.00 EUR	0.00 EUR
1000 Land and similar rig	10,000,000.00 EUR	0.00 EUR
Accumulated depreciation	1,060,128.39- EUR	1,156,918.00- EUR
1010 ADP - real estate	1,060,128.39- EUR	1,156,918.00- EUR
Plant and machinery	221,844.73- EUR	270,543.00 EUR
Acquisition value	90,480.00 EUR	500,000.00 EUR
11000 Machinery and equip.	90,480.00 EUR	500,000.00 EUR
Accumulated depreciation	312,324.73- EUR	229,457.00- EUR
11010 ADP-mach./equipment	312,324.73- EUR	229,457.00- EUR
Other fixtures and fitings,	28,133.00- EUR	84,299.00- EUR
Accumulated depreciation	28,133.00- EUR	84,299.00- EUR
21010 ADP - fixts/fittgs	28,133.00- EUR	84,299.00- EUR

ii) Report for Reconciliation Accounts

S_ALR_87012279 Structured Account Balances

Reconciliation accounts are the GL accounts that interface with Asset Accounting, Accounts Receivable, and Accounts Payable modules.

We may be interested in extracting the standard reports for specific reconciliation accounts. For example, when we work with Fixed Assets related entries, we may be interested in a report of all GL accounts that interface with the Asset Accounting module.

We can extract the Asset Accounting interfacing GL accounts by selecting 'A' under the 'Dynamic Selections >> Company Code >> Recon. Account' for the account type.

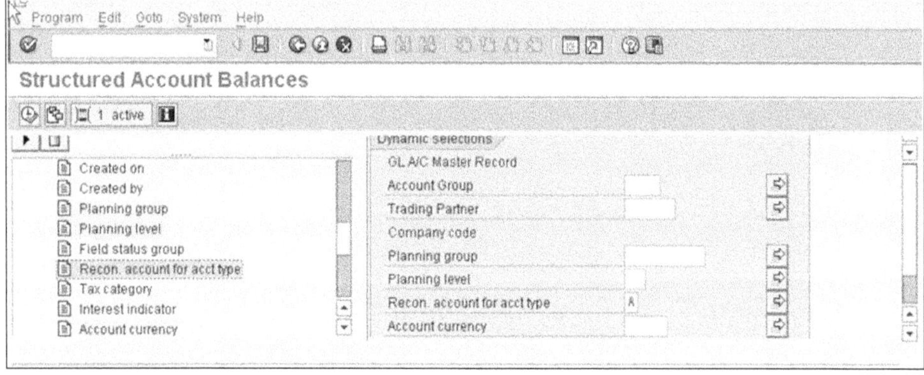

iii) Report for Tax Accounts

S_ALR_87012279 Structured Account Balances

We may have more than one input tax accounts, such as CGST Input Tax, SGST Input Tax, IGST Input Tax.

We can extract the system report for all such input tax accounts by choosing '<' under the Dynamic Selections >> Company Code >> Tax Category

Choose '>' sign to get the output tax accounts report.

iv) Report for Foreign Currency GL Accounts

S_ALR_87012279 Structured Account Balances

We can get a report of GL accounts maintained in a foreign currency.

Consider your CC code currency is INR, and you have one or more GL accounts in USD currency.

You can extract a report of only USD currency by selecting USD in Dynamic Selections: Company Code >> Account Currency.

v) Report by Customers City and Postal Code

S_ALR_87012172 Customer Balances in Local Currency

Main Menu: Edit >> Dynamic Selections: Customer Master >> City and Postal Code

In dynamic selections, we can select the customers by city and postal code.

vi) Report by Customer Business Group

S_ALR_87012172 Customer Balances in Local Currency

We can define customer or vendor groups in the system. As an illustration, you have three customer accounts, all belonging to **one business group**. Now, we are interested in extracting the report S_ALR_87012172 Customer Balances report for all three customer accounts together.

We can do so by selecting Dynamic Selections >> Customer Master >> Group Key.

Please refer to the topic Defining Corporate Groups (page no. 35) under Chapter 4 AR & AP Master Record Key Parameters, discussing how to create and use group keys.

vii) Report by Customers Account Group

S_ALR_87012172 Customer Balances in Local Currency

Account group is the classification & grouping of similar customers or vendors' accounts.

For example, the system configuration for customer account groups may be:

1) Domestic Customers
2) Foreign Customers
3) One Time Customers

We can get a report for the 'domestic customers' by selecting Dynamic Selections >> Customer Master >> Account Group: Domestic Customers.

viii) Report by Customer VAT Registration Number

Dynamic Selections: Customer Master >> VAT Registration no.

We have the VAT Registration number, and we want to know if any customer account matches the specific VAT /GST number. It is an excellent test to avoid customer account duplication when we create a new customer account.

We can run a report S_ALR_87012172 Customer Balances to determine if that customer account already exists.

ix) Report for Customers Assigned to an Accounting Clerk

Consider you are responsible for a particular set of customer accounts. Then you get the system report S_ALR_87012172 Customer Balances only for customers for whom you are responsible using:

> 'Dynamic Selections: Company Code >> Accounting Clerk: (Accounting Clerk code).'

Please refer to Assigning Master Records to Accounting Clerks (page no. 34) under Chapter 4 AR & AP Master Record Key Parameters discussing how to assign accounting clerks to customers' and vendors' accounts.

∞

10. Background Processing

As we work with the SAP System, we often encounter scenarios when the system suggests choosing **'Background Processing.'**

We know the system requires resources to execute the queries we pose to the system. Some of the queries that we want to run are resource intense. We can optimize the system resource utilization by following a simple protocol, using background processing for resource-intense queries.

Background processing improves system performance. The system gives you options to execute the background tasks during off-peak hours.

Which tasks do you have to assign background processing?

You don't have to worry. Whenever you execute a substantial resource-consuming transaction, the system will respond with a message suggesting you go for background processing.

For example, when we have numerous assets in our 'fixed assets' portfolio, running the monthly 'depreciation posting run' is a system intense program.

Once you select the TCode for the depreciation posting run, the system prompts us as 'Online, the processing is limited to approximately 1000 assets'

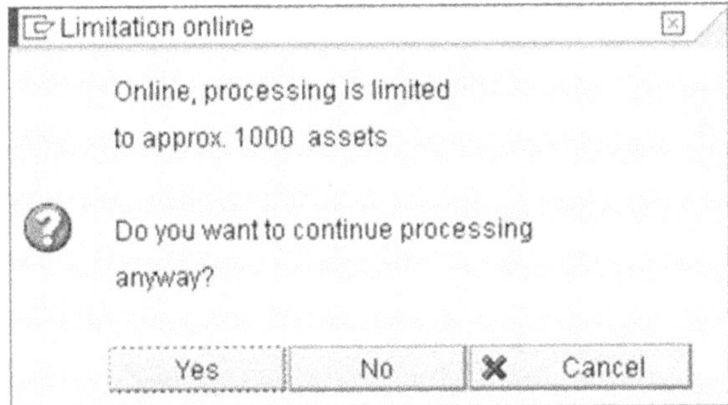

When we have assets exceeding 1000 in numbers, we choose the 'No' option and go to the Main Menu to execute the depreciation run program in the background.

Main Menu: Program >> Execute in Background

The system prompts you to select the printer. Once the printer is set, we can schedule the background job date and time.

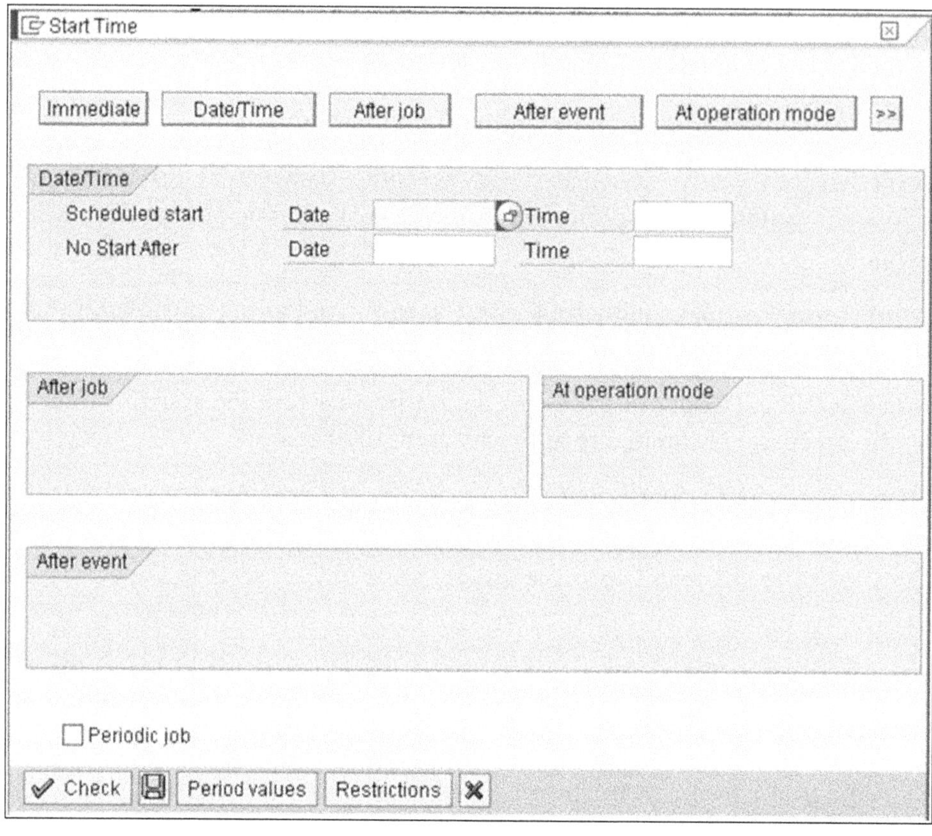
Start Time
Immediate
Date/Time
After job
After event
At operation mode
>>
Date/Time
Scheduled start
Date
Time
No Start After
Date
Time
After job
At operation mode
After event
Periodic job
Check
Period values
Restrictions

Background Processes Status

Main Menu: System >> Services >> Batch Input >> Sessions

You'll find the list of Batch Input sessions created.

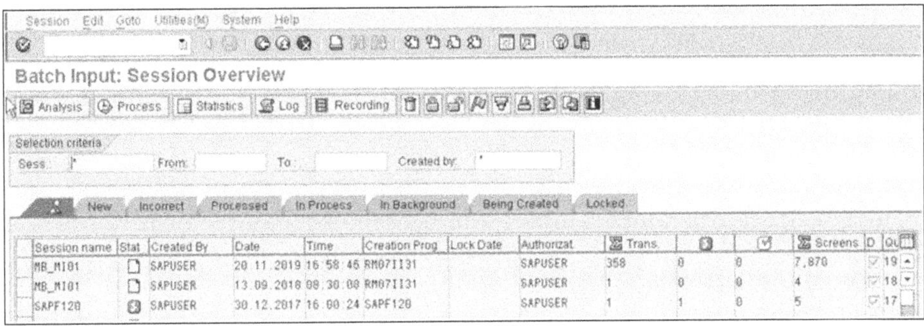

The column 'status' indicates status like New, Errors, In Processing, etc. We can select the session when the status is **'New'** and click the button **'Process,'** and choose 'Process Background.'

When the background processing is complete, the system will display transactions posted without errors and the number of transactions not posted due to errors.

We can select the transactions with **'Error'** status and process them in the **'Foreground'** mode. Processing in 'foreground mode' walks us through each step of the transaction processing. Thus, we can understand the reasons for the error and make the corrections.

∞∞

Author's Endnote

Congratulations on completing the SAP Financial Accounting.

I have made every effort to make the subject as simple as possible and cover it as wide as necessary to help you succeed as an SAP Accountant.

I wish you the very best in your career using SAP FICO.

∞∞∞

Thank You for Reading

I have tried my level best to make 'SAP Financial Accounting' a comprehensive study for an SAP Accountant.

Have you found this book helpful? Has it delivered what it promised? In case if you are not satisfied, be kind to send me a note at murugesan0202@yahoo.com.

If you have enjoyed reading this book and feel benefited, please leave your honest comments and ratings.

As an author, I read every comment, and it helps me improve this book.

You may leave your honest comments on the amazon page (links below) or the store from where you bought the book.

USA https://bit.ly/sapfi675
India https://bit.ly/sap_fi685
UK https://bit.ly/sapfi695

Your few words of appreciation mean so much to me!

Your pal,

Murugesan Ramaswamy :)

ထထ

Join Facebook Group

The author of this book invites you to join the Facebook group to raise your doubts and share your experience and knowledge with fellow SAP Accountants and Finance Managers. He will also pitch in to share his knowledge.

Follow the link to join today:

https://sapficouser.com/home/facebook-group/

∞∞

Other Titles by the Author

Book 1 in SAP FICO Books

SAP FICO Beginner's Handbook

This is the first book in the SAP FICO books series. This book is for absolute beginners with SAP FICO.

The book explains SAP FICO modules concepts to guide you to improve productivity using SAP FICO. Follow the link to know more about and order the book: https://sapficouser.com/home/sapficobooks/

∞∞

Finance for Non-financial Managers

FNFMS book is a quick reference finance handbook to learn how to read and interpret financial statements. You will also learn the core financial concepts explained in simple language.

To know more about the book or order the book, please follow the link: https://sapficouser.com/finance-books/

∞∞

Connect with the Author

You can contact the author at: murugesan0202@yahoo.com, admin@sapficouser.com

For updates on new releases & subscribing to SAP FICO USER News Letter, please visit: https://sapficouser.com

THANK YOU FOR YOUR SUPPORT!

∞∞∞

www.ingramcontent.com/pod-product-compliance
Ingram Content Group UK Ltd.
Pitfield, Milton Keynes, MK11 3LW, UK
UKHW061701190726
13853UKWH00008B/2350